WHAT
RUSTY
TAUGHT ME ABOUT GOD

CHUCK HESTER

ISBN 979-8-89309-719-1 (Paperback)
ISBN 979-8-89309-720-7 (Digital)

All biblical citations were taken from the English Standard Version of the Holy Bible unless otherwise indicated.

Covenant Books
11661 Hwy 707
Murrells Inlet, SC 29576
www.covenantbooks.com

CONTENTS

MY TESTIMONY

I know this is a book about my dog, and I promise to stay true to the subject for the rest of the endeavor. However, none of it will make sense unless I tell you *my* story first.

I grew up in church. In fact, I can't recall a time when I didn't attend regularly—such was the devotion of my parents. This was typical and even socially expected in a small town like Geraldine, Alabama.

We moved to Geraldine when I was three years old. The people who sold us the house in the middle of town invited us to the First Baptist Church just up the street. We started attending, and it even served as the place for both kindergarten and Sunday school.

My religious education was thorough. I learned the stories—Adam and Eve, Daniel and the lion's den, Noah's ark—all the standards. I also learned about Jesus. He was the baby in the manger at Christmas. He turned water into wine. (As a Southern Baptist, I was very confused about that one.) At Easter, we heard about His crucifixion, death, and resurrection—but I had no idea what all of that had to do with me.

Then I heard about being saved. It seemed to be something I was expected to do, and it also appeared to involve going to the front of the church during the invitation hymn (most likely "I Surrender All" or "Just As I Am"). For an introverted child, the prospect was a bit terrifying.

While I was at a Bible camp one summer, we had an emotional, week-ending altar call. My friends went forward, so I followed. I had no idea what was going on, but I seemed to be making everyone happy and proud. My parents must have suspected the fakeness of my profession of faith, as they didn't pressure me to be baptized.

Years passed, and we had a revival at church. Revivals are occasional week-long programs that involve a visiting preacher as well as special musical offerings from various performers. Billy Graham was saved at just such a service. The music that night featured a praise band, which was a welcome departure from the piano and organ accompaniment to which we were accustomed. There were drums, guitars, and contemporary-style lyrics delivered by hippie-looking vocalists. I was enthralled. In fact, they overshadowed the sermon, which I can't recall at all. Once again, my emotions were swayed.

By this point, I knew about heaven—where I wanted to go—and hell—where I did not want to go. Getting "saved" seemed like a sort of safety net.

During the invitation, our preacher, Charles Jones, got up and said, "If you ask God to save you, He'll do it." That sounded like a great deal to me, so once again, I went forward. This time, I knelt and asked God to save me.

I clearly remember my dad saying, "Son, I got saved when I was ten years old, and I've never once regretted it." Once again, everyone seemed happy and proud of me.

The following day, my dad took me back to the church, where I talked to the preacher alone. I must have smiled and nodded in all the correct places because he assured me that this time I really was saved.

The problem was that no real conversion took place. I thought the reason God forgave our sins was because He was nice. I associated being a Christian with something earned by good behavior. I had no understanding of why Jesus died on the cross or what it meant to surrender to His Lordship, but I can't blame anyone for this. God alone decides when a person is ready to understand these things.

Time, as the song says, marches on.

In 1981, my father died. My brothers and sisters were adults by this time, but I was a very immature twelve-year-old. In some ways, I've never really gotten over it. Maybe it's like that for everyone. Dad was the leader of our family unit, a pillar of the community, and the music director at the church. He was the band director at Geraldine High School from 1969 to 1978, so hundreds of kids had also seen him as a father figure. My mother was understandably devastated, as were my grandparents and siblings. He had been my rock, but now he was gone. You may as well have told me that the sky was green instead of blue. Was anything real? Did anything last? The devil took full advantage of these thoughts and planted seeds of doubt in my mind regarding the existence of God. These I kept to myself.

I continued to attend church, went to youth camps, and sang in the choir. However, I really only did those things to placate my mother. Then one day, I simply stopped.

The hypocrisy was just too much, so I began—at age sixteen—to live what I believed: religion was a farce meant to calm the fear of death. Bible stories were just that—stories. I would live according to my conscience and establish a life based on my own ideas of morality. In short, I would become my own god.

John wrote about people like this. In 1 John 2:18–19, he called them "antichrists" and said that by leaving the faith, they had proven that they had never really believed. That was me. I was an antichrist and an enemy of God, as referenced in James 4:4. It's not that I lost salvation. I never had it. If my story stopped there, I would be in hell today.

God had other plans.

In fact, He had a lot of plans. In hindsight, I can see that He was setting me up for the most important decision of my life.

In 1990, I married Tina Roden, whom I'd met while working in a local grocery store called Foodland. It was a tale as old as time: a whirlwind romance between cashier and bagger. Later, she went on to a career at the town bank, while I found employment at Sara Lee, a commercial bakery in Fort Payne. I was working there when our children were born. Zach arrived in 1993, and Jada followed in 1998.

I loved my family dearly, but I failed as a father during their formative years. I was lost, and Tina, whom I had never known to be religious, started taking them to church.

I didn't mind the fact that they were attending. The cute Bible stories were good for children, and I was happy to allow Tina to take on the role of our family's spiritual leader. Besides, I worked the third shift on the weekends. The need for sleep superseded my desire to go to church.

On the rare occasion when I accompanied them to church, the experience freaked me out. The pastor was a heavyset young man who screamed rather than preached his sermons. He sweated, slobbered, and his entire head turned purple. The congregation whooped, cheered, and shouted, "Amen!"

All this was a far cry from the tranquil, perhaps stuffy, atmosphere of the church in which I grew up. The result was a further entrenchment in agnosticism.

Tina eventually decided that the kids needed Sunday school, which was offered for all ages at Geraldine First

Baptist Church. God then began to use my children to draw me to Himself.

"Why doesn't Daddy go with us?" Zach would inquire.

I didn't really have an answer that my family would understand, so I went along.

I was surprised to find the people were friendly and welcoming, and I was still technically a member. Sunday school turned out to be interesting. People were studying and discussing the Bible, and the pastor's sermons seemed applicable to life. My heart started to soften.

Then, on one Sunday in September, a few weeks after the 9/11 terrorist attacks, God made His move.

I can't remember the lesson or scripture passage we studied that morning. It could have been Romans 5:8, which says, "but God shows his love for us in that while we were still sinners, Christ died for us." If it wasn't that, then it must have been something similar.

"If it wasn't for Jesus Christ doing what He did, we would have no hope." That's what I can recall the teacher saying that day.

It was a simple message. I'm sure I'd heard it before, yet it shook me to my core. I barely remember walking from the class to the sanctuary for the worship service. I can't remember the sermon topic or the hymns that we sang. That simple statement played over and over again in my head, and suddenly, I was faced with a decision. Either the people surrounding me were idiots worshipping a false story, in which case I should get up, take my family, and leave, or it was all true. That would mean that Jesus Christ really was—and is—the Son of God who loved me enough to face torture and death to atone for my sins. In that case, I owed Him my heart and my life.

It was a weird and wonderful moment as time seemed to halt. I felt like there was no one else in the sanctuary besides God and me.

I couldn't ride the fence any longer. In fact, I realized the fence of indecision didn't actually exist and that God was demanding that I make a choice: *up or down? Yes or no? Right or left? Believe or reject?*

I chose to believe as something inside me broke in surrender to His offer. My prayer was simple: *Okay.* Which meant I was placing my faith in Jesus to atone for my sins and giving my life to His Lordship. I can't really describe the feelings that I experienced except to say that they were more than emotions. It was a weight lifted, a hope of a second chance, and a sure knowledge that something wonderful had transpired.

Because I grew up in church, I was familiar with the church terminology. At the time, I thought of this as a rededication. However, I also realized that I had never experienced anything like this. 1 John 4:19 says that we love God because He first loved us, and that was exactly how I felt. I was so filled with love and gratitude for what Jesus had done for me that I sought to completely give myself over to Him.

I finally realized why He had called the process "born again" (John 3:3).

Everything changed.

Where I had once felt bitter and mistrustful of Christians, I now view them as brothers and sisters. I began to see the work of the church—spreading the gospel—as the most important thing anyone could ever do. I suddenly saw the Bible as more than a collection of stories—it seemed to come alive. I looked forward to studying it, and I found that I could relate to the people in its pages. I looked forward to prayer. This was time alone with God when I could bare my soul to Him and confess my sins.

Speaking of sin, I began to see it as God saw it.

I repented when it crept back into my habits. Naturally, sin did and always will have an appeal, but my love for Jesus was such that I didn't want to practice it anymore.

I wish I could say that I became perfect, but every day, I still rely on God's grace and forgiveness. I'm a work in progress.

God didn't just remove various sins from my life; He gave much more than He took, and the most important gift was a desire and talent for teaching. Teaching required me to study, and study led to growth. The first time I taught was in Vacation Bible School. Then He opened doors for me to teach different age groups in Sunday school classes.

That's when God began to use our dog, a now fifteen-year-old dachshund named Rusty, to illustrate biblical truths in lessons as well as in my personal life.

It's the same teaching style that Jesus used in His parables. He used understandable, common experiences to teach deep spiritual facts. Jesus is our example in all things, including teaching style, so He eventually inspired me to write some of the lessons He taught me through Rusty.

If God can use Balaam's donkey, then what's to stop Him from using Chuck's dachshund?

The stories you'll find next aren't perfect. They might even be misquoted. However, they're important conversations and situations that I remember to the best of my recollection and that formed me as a person. Or, as I stated earlier, a work in progress.

WHAT YOU THINK
YOU WANT

It was the fall of 2008. Tina and I were enjoying a rare bit of alone time running errands when she said something that took me by surprise.

"I've been thinking about what to get the kids for Christmas," she said. "They really want a dog."

"Really"? I responded doubtfully.

We had tried owning a dog once before after moving from our country home in Skirum to the town of Crossville. It hadn't ended well.

Buzzy was a rescue pet, a labrador mixed with other various breeds, and while mutts usually make good pets, the move to a subdivision was problematic for her. She had become accustomed to roaming the countryside freely, but after the move, she was confined to a small, fenced backyard. We were afraid to let her out of the fence because of the dangerous traffic as well as her constant threats toward the neighbor's flower beds. Not to mention the strays that populated the neighborhood. Labradors are smart dogs, so they get bored easily. To pass the time, Buzzy began to chew the siding off the house!

Something had to give, so we made the heart-wrenching decision to leave her in the care of our former Skirum neighbors, where she would be much happier. Jada, on the other hand, was not happy. Listening to her cry on the way home nearly killed me, and I had no desire to relive that experience.

"Yeah," she continued. "I was thinking about a small dog."

I instantly formed a mental image of just the kind of dog I wanted.

"You mean like a Chihuahua?" I asked.

"No," she replied. "A dachshund."

In retrospect, the kids had been talking about dachshunds for a while. They are small dogs with long bodies and stubby legs and are commonly known as "wiener dogs."

My mental image shifted accordingly.

"Oh, okay. I like the black and tan ones. They look like mischievous little bandits wearing masks."

"No," she dismissed. "A red one."

We had been married for eighteen years, and as is the case in any marriage, we had had our share of disagreements. Experience has given me a modicum of husbandly wisdom, namely that there are some hills not worth dying on. Besides, I wanted a dog just as much as the kids did. I also realized that getting a dog of any breed was a huge concession on Tina's part, as she didn't really care for pets.

"Sure," I agreed. "That's just what I always wanted—a red wiener dog."

Life is like that. We form ideas about what and when we want it, and we leave God and His good, pleasing, and perfect will—as described in Romans 12:2—out of our plans. (Actually, we have no guarantee that we will even live to see them come to fruition. James 4:13–16 denounces this sort of presumptuous mindset.) It's not that getting a dog was wrong for us, but Buzzy had been the wrong dog at the wrong time. The Bible is replete with examples of people with well-intended ideas that flopped because either God was not the catalyst for the idea or the timing was wrong.

Moses is the perfect example. God's people were slaves in Egypt, but Moses, because of God's provision, was raised in the Pharaoh's palace. Despite his royal upbringing, he still saw himself as a Hebrew. Exodus 2:11–14 tells us how Moses decided, without any instruction from God, to come to the aid of one of his fellow Hebrews who was being beaten by an Egyptian. Moses killed the Egyptian and hid the body, but his plan backfired when the murder became known. Fearing for his life, Moses fled to Midian, where he lived for the next forty years. He married there and became a shepherd. (How's that for a time out?) Of course, none of this surprised God, who had His own perfect plan to deliver His people, but it had to be done in His way and in His timing. Moses thought small, delivering one Hebrew from one Egyptian. God thought big and long-term. His plan was to free an entire nation. The remainder of the book of Exodus explains how God, through Moses, accomplished that liberation.

A New Testament example of this same simple truth appears in John 6:1–15.

Jesus was healing and teaching, activities that drew a large crowd, but those in attendance needed something to eat. They couldn't simply send them home for fear that they would faint from hunger on the way. His disciples began to fret about how to feed so many people until a little boy offered to share his lunch: five barley loaves and two fish. It wasn't much, but it was all he had to offer. The disciples began to talk about how few people it could feed. They thought small. The Lord thought big.

He blessed it, broke it, and proceeded to feed over five thousand people with it! The crowd was overwhelmed and overjoyed by this miraculous lunch.

Their response was an attempt to make Jesus their king. Perhaps He would be a great warrior like David. Maybe He could drive the Romans out of Israel. Finally, they could be free! Again, we see man's disregard for the will and timing of God. They were thinking of an earthly kingdom and freedom from the Roman occupation of Israel. God's plan was freedom from the consequences of sin, as explained in John 3:16, and an eternal kingdom.

Don't be quick to pass judgment on Moses or on this crowd. When we notice the shortcomings of biblical characters, God is usually making us aware of the same sin in our own lives. So often, I'm just like these people in that I think I know what I want and need. I pray for these things and become downhearted or even angry when I don't get the answer that I expect; however, as God patiently grows me, I'm discovering that He is doing more through my suffering and waiting than I could ever ask or imagine. The book of James also explains this fact in chapter 1, verses 2 and 3: "Count it all joy, my brothers, when you meet trials of various kinds, for you know that the testing of your faith produces steadfastness."

That's easy to teach in a comfortable Sunday school classroom while nothing is going wrong in your life, but untested faith isn't really faith at all. I would experience this lesson firsthand beginning in the summer of 2017, when I decided, at the age of forty-nine, to join a gym.

It had been years since I had attempted any type of structured exercise regimen. Instead, I relied on my job to provide me with all the physical activity I needed. Whether it was the grocery store, bakery, assembly line, or postal service, my employment had always involved rigorous physical labor. This made me feel like an underachieving loser because I had been a teenager in the "Yuppie" era of the 1980s, when we were encouraged to seek "professional" careers, preferably parked behind a desk. This mindset had led to a couple of wasted years attending a local community college, where my lack of focus was evident in my grades. Eventually, I lost interest and dropped out.

Defeated, I simply "got on" with the rest of my life: jobs, marriage, kids, mortgage, etc. I was oblivious, even after my salvation, to the fact that God was quietly working behind the scenes.

One evening, I was at the gym doing dumbbell curls with my right arm when I noticed a twitch in my left thumb. I thought this was curious but not alarming.

Over the next few months, the twitch progressed into a shake, which later happened even when I was at rest. I chose to ignore it for years, even though it was obviously getting worse, dismissing it as a nerve problem or perhaps just overworked muscles.

Finally, the shaking began to interfere with my quality of life.

My work became more challenging. Leading music or teaching Sunday school, activities that I loved, were now tainted with worry about people watching my arm. Any situation that would make a normal person tremble would make me shake rapidly. I grew stressed, anxious, and depressed. These were issues with which I had previously struggled, but now they are amplified. I sought help from my chiropractor, but adjustments didn't seem to make any difference in my condition. My regular physician suggested that it was an affliction called essential tremors and prescribed beta blockers. These made me feel loopy without helping the shaking. She referred me to a neurologist.

On the day of my first appointment, I had no idea what to expect. The waiting room was dimly lit, and the nurses station was shielded by plexiglass. The COVID-19 pandemic was terrorizing the globe, so masks were strictly required. I sat and waited alone, unfrightened.

After all, how bad could it be?

My name was called. I was led to an examination room, where I waited even more. I began to feel anxious, and the shaking started to flare up in my left hand. I simply wanted to get my diagnosis and go home. At last, the neurologist entered and introduced herself. She was a tall, blond lady with a foreign name and accent that reminded me of Natasha from the Rocky and Bullwinkle cartoons.

I kept those thoughts to myself, as a nervous sense of humor isn't always appreciated. Instead of a clinical test, she observed my shaking, listened to my list of symptoms, and put me through a series of motions, not unlike a drunk test one might experience on the side of the interstate at the behest of a state trooper. I watched as she made notes and checked off a list.

Then came the diagnosis: I had Parkinson's disease.

I was incredulous. The worst I had expected was some type of shoulder or neck surgery. I couldn't have Parkinson's! The shock was comparable to the feelings I experienced the morning I lost my dad, as my world seemed to turn upside down. These things were supposed to happen to other people, not to me. Visions of Michael J. Fox and his obvious decline sprang to mind. I felt so healthy. What about my plans for retirement? What if Tina had to care for me as my health deteriorated?

I could barely breathe, let alone listen as she attempted to educate me about the disease—*my disease*. She explained that there is no medical test that can conclusively diagnose Parkinson's. There is no cure. We can only treat the symptoms. She went on to explain how the medicines worked and scheduled an MRI to rule out the possibility of a brain tumor. She told me it was impossible to predict the rate of progression. She told me how some people lose the ability to walk. (She was a real ray of sunshine.) She told me some people can control the symptoms for a time with medication. She even explained a procedure performed at a hospital in Birmingham that involves a device implanted *in the patient's brain* to regulate the flow of dopamine. (Insufficient dopamine levels associated with the disease cause tremors.)

She seemed almost cheerful as she drove the nails into my coffin.

I checked out, made an appointment for the MRI, and then, as I grabbed the door handle, I froze. If I walked out the door, it would become real. I prayed for strength and stepped into the sunshine, where I called Tina to tell her the news. I tried to act brave, but inside, I was a wreck. Where was the peace I was supposed to feel? I called my family when I got home, telling them the news. I was starting to freak out a little at this point. Some tried to console me. Some suggested that I take up smoking marijuana. One of them pragmatically told me, "Well, we're all gonna die of something someday." I called my pastor, who prayed for me over the phone and offered to put out a churchwide call on my behalf. I declined, as I was already tired of pity. Telling my mother was the worst, because for some inexplicable reason, I felt that I was disappointing her.

The MRI results showed no tumor or other abnormality, so I began taking medication. When that didn't stop the tremors, she increased my dosage. The tremors lessened slightly, but not completely. I got a second opinion, but he agreed with the diagnosis and course of treatment.

The whole thing seemed like quackery. They were all saying things like, "Let's try this or that and see what happens." It's no wonder they call it "practicing medicine."

I went into full denial mode, forsaking both medicine and doctors. The depression worsened, as did the anxiety. Most of the time I could mask this, but inwardly, I began to wonder what it would be like to just lay down and die peacefully. I felt guilty for feeling this way, and I knew that I couldn't cause my family such pain, nor did I want to sin against God. The trapped feeling caused more anxiety, which in turn caused more shaking.

Everything came to a head during a vacation in Gatlinburg, where the family always spent Thanksgiving week.

I was recovering from a case of COVID while we lodged at a hotel. Vacations are supposed to relax a person; instead, I began to feel even more stressed. The shaking became unstoppable. My left arm and shoulder cramped and ached. I laid down to sleep, but when rest wouldn't come, I went into a full-blown panic attack. I got up. I tried to read. I paced the floors. Again, I wanted to die.

It was at this point that God showed me just how much my wife loved me. She got out of bed too. She didn't try to "talk me down." She just sat up with me, making sure that I was okay. Finally, after a generous slug of my cough syrup, I was able to sleep. The next morning, I called my regular physician, who prescribed medication to take the edge off for the rest of the trip.

After we returned home, I was determined to make changes. I got a prescription for Lexapro and trazodone. These helped with anxiety and insomnia. I took a break from teaching Sunday school, and God showed me how much my church family loved me as someone graciously volunteered to fill in during the hiatus.

I got advice from Keith Swisher, another Parkinson's patient, who attended my church and became an invaluable prayer partner to me. He also recommended his doctor at UAB, where he was on the waiting list for the deep brain stimulation implant that my first neurologist had described.

I learned that people from all over the southeast seek UAB for their various neurological maladies. Feeling cautiously optimistic, I made the appointment, but this time would be different. Tina accompanied me as we decided to face the challenge together.

I discovered that UAB is not just one hospital building.

In fact, the campus seems to sprawl all over Birmingham. Our appointment was in a building called the Kirkland Clinic, where the bulk of their neurological medicine is practiced.

The neurologist was a pleasant young man, and the facilities and staff were modern and professional. He confirmed the diagnosis and, like the other two doctors, put me through a battery of coordination and strength tests. He repeated much of what I already knew about my disease (no cure, characterized by a lack of dopamine, and progression rates vary from person to person). Then he explained some facts that I didn't know.

As Parkinson's patients go, I was lucky.

I wasn't hallucinating or thrashing in my sleep. I wasn't "spacing out." Compared with other neurological diseases, Parkinson's was much less debilitating than ALS or Alzheimer's.

"I see other people come in here all the time with far worse problems than Parkinson's, and I have to tell them, 'I know what's wrong with you, but there isn't a damn thing I can do about it,'" he said. "But we can get you some relief from your symptoms."

"For real?" I said hopefully. "You can help with this?" I gestured to my rhythmically shaking left arm.

"Absolutely."

He went on to explain the deep brain stimulation more in depth and how my condition would deteriorate as the disease inevitably progressed, making the surgery a future necessity. (My Parkinson's buddy at church would eventually have this procedure and enjoy great success.) While I had already heard these things, I never really accepted them, but I finally realized that it was time to step out of denial. I had to stop running. I would, with God's help, learn to live with this. I had given Him my life, and that included this left arm. If He wanted it to shake, then He must have a good reason for that. The doctor then told me something that caused me to marvel at the wisdom and omnipotence of God.

"I recommend 150 minutes of exercise per week," he told me. "And I see that you already go to the gym. Your job as a mailman probably also helps keep you fit."

"Sure," I answered. "I've always had physically demanding jobs, requiring me to stay in shape by walking, bending, stretching, lifting, and carrying heavy loads."

"And that," he declared, "is why your symptoms are still relatively mild. If you had worked behind a desk and led a sedentary life, you would be in far worse shape. There's currently no drug that can slow this disease, but regular exercise can."

I was astounded. For all of my adult life, I have berated myself for not finishing college. I thought myself a loser and a failure, but what I thought I wanted and needed (a desk job) was the farthest thing from what was actually best for me. God had been in control the whole time, placing me exactly where I needed to be because He knew the challenges I would face. In His love, He protected me from my own desires. It was the same way that I had thought I wanted a black and tan Chihuahua when what I really needed was a red wiener dog.

When I consider all the logistics of arranging one path in one life, I am amazed. I can't even begin to imagine how He does it in every situation in every life. There must be a thousand near misses in one average day of my existence. He's constantly watching and protecting me. The Bible tells us that He knows when a sparrow falls and that the hairs on our heads are numbered. Maybe when I'm with Him in heaven, He'll tell me about all the times that He stepped in to save me from myself, and will He laugh? I just might.

Choosing Rusty

We make choices every day. Some are inconsequential: Should I wear a blue shirt or a red one? Do I want Mexican or Chinese food for lunch? Other choices are more serious and life-changing: Should I look for a job in Huntsville or Birmingham? Should I buy a house or continue to rent?

Sometimes the choices are all about timing: When should I get married? When should I have children? Sometimes, however, what seems like a small choice turns out to be very life-altering. Such was the case when Tina chose Rusty.

We wanted a red dachshund, and with a wife who knows everyone in Geraldine, finding a breeder was easy. An older couple named Richard and Tina Maddox lived on the outskirts of town, raised miniature dachshunds (eleven pounds and under), and would have a litter ready for adoption by Christmas Day.

The puppies were reasonably priced because they weren't AKC registered, but we didn't care about pedigree papers. We wanted a pet, not a sire, so when they were around two weeks old, Tina paid them a visit and made her choice.

The little fur babies were asleep in a small enclosure, but even if they had been awake, it would have been impossible to judge things like temperament or intelligence as they were so tiny, and their eyes could barely open. Still, they were impossibly cute and utterly helpless. She fell in love with one in particular.

"That one," she said, peering into their world, and pointed to the little rusty red pup. "I want him."

Money was paid, and hands were shaken. Rusty continued to snore blissfully, unaware that Tina's choice would change the entire course of his life and ours.

Tina came home excited to tell me about our newly adopted "child." Again, I was surprised at her newfound interest in a pet. Perhaps it had something to do with the fact that our kids were growing up rapidly. She needed something to cuddle with (besides me). I was excited but also a little nervous, fearing that somehow it wouldn't work out. It took all my willpower to keep our secret until Christmas Eve, when we went to pick him up.

I had never seen the house before that night, nor had I met the couple. I wasn't really sure what to expect. Dog breeders have gotten a bad reputation lately, probably because of the ASPCA commercials showing cold, starving animals in tiny cages. While that is an accurate portrayal in some cases, the Maddox home was nothing like that. We arrived at a lovely brick house decorated for Christmas, with the shrubbery tastefully strewn with lights. Upon entering, we could see that the interior was also festively prepared for Christmas, complete with a tree in the corner and a fire crackling in the hearth. A miniature schnauzer sat contentedly on Richard's lap. They both seemed engrossed in *A Christmas Story* playing on TBS. Tina, his wife, not mine, offered a quick lesson on puppy ownership.

"I've already separated it from the others," she said. I found it curious that she chose *it* to describe the puppy rather than *him*, and I wondered if that was to keep herself from getting too attached to them.

"It's been eating dry food, and I've packed some for you in a ziplock bag," she said. "You may have a hard time getting it to eat for a couple of days until it gets used to its new surroundings. It has no sphincter control at this age, so it eats and then almost immediately poops."

How charming, I thought.

She said Rusty would cry for a few nights, and we'd go without sleep.

"It's not crying for its mother," she assured us. "It's crying for its littermates because it's not used to sleeping alone."

My mind began to wander to my childhood experiences of dog ownership and how those puppies whimpered for the first few nights. Of course, those were outside dogs, whereas this little fellow would be in our house!

This was beginning to sound like a lot of work. Were we ready for this?

We left with our little rust-colored bundle of joy in a small cardboard box covered with, you guessed it, a receiving blanket. We were somewhat sobered, but we had made our choice. The die was cast, and we were still excited to introduce him to the kids. This present definitely would not wait until Christmas morning.

Our children were ten and fifteen years old, but everyone turns into a three-year-old at the sight of a new puppy. They were no exception.

"Is it a dog? It's a dog, isn't it?" Zach babbled excitedly when he saw the box.

"He's so cute!" Jada squealed.

"What's his name?" They asked almost in unison. Tina and I had discussed this in advance. We were looking forward to a long relationship with this dog, and we didn't want to invite a situation that involved us yelling, "Commander Wiggles, come here, boy."

Tina had offered me the choice of either Darby or Rusty. I opted for simplicity, and the rest is history.

"His name is Rusty," we said, and the kids agreed that the name suited him. We stayed up late playing with him. Never had a puppy been so thoroughly welcomed and enjoyed. Rusty was the star attraction that year. Come to think of it, no Christmas before or since has come close to comparison.

If you are a born-again believer then this scenario sounds very familiar to you. You are the puppy, and God—in a time and for a purpose of His own choosing—looked down into our small world and said, *I want him.* Just as we were overjoyed to welcome Rusty to our family, the Bible tells us that there is joy in heaven over one sinner who comes to repentance.

This is incredible for several reasons. The first of which is that God does the choosing. In John 15:16, Jesus said to His disciples, "You did not choose me, but I chose you and appointed you that you should go and bear fruit and that your fruit should abide." This means that nobody can choose to do anything genuinely good apart from God. Furthermore, nobody chooses the timing of his salvation.

So often, we share the gospel with a lost person only to hear them say that they believe what we're saying but that they're not ready to commit right now. They'll do it *someday*, as though they're postponing gallbladder surgery. Perhaps on their deathbed, they'll get saved after living life on their terms. This plan is seriously flawed.

For starters, not everyone gets a deathbed. Your death may come swiftly from a car crash or a heart attack. In fact, James 4:13–16 tells us that it is presumptuous and prideful to make any plans apart from God's will and timing. He writes that our lives are "vapor" in that they vanish quickly. Secondly, if a person really believes that Jesus is who He says He is—the one and only Son of God—that He did what He says He did (died as an atoning sacrifice for our sins) and will do what He says He'll do (give us new life both now and eternally), then that person will not be content to remain lost for another second. Lastly, in Matthew 8:21–22, Jesus rebuked those whom He invited to follow Him when they replied that they had other things to do first. Jesus will not settle for second place. That means He is not only our savior. He is also our Lord.

However, this does not mean that His offer of salvation by faith through grace is "irresistible," as the Calvinist doctrine claims. In fact, people resist Him every day. That's where the analogy of a lost soul to Rusty ends. Rusty had no choice in the matter of his adoption. Mankind does have a choice.

In Matthew 23:37, Jesus laments over Jerusalem, saying that He had wanted to gather them as a mother hen gathers her chicks. He revealed that the reason He hadn't done so was due to the fact that they weren't willing. He never mentioned anything about them not being predestined. Furthermore, in John chapter 3, during His conversation with a Pharisee named Nicodemus, Jesus stated that **"whoever"** would believe in Him would not perish but have eternal life. The one who did not believe would remain condemned. This means that we have a choice in the matter of our salvation. God chooses us, but He also gives us the freedom to decline Him. This is perfectly logical and fair. After all, forced love isn't really love at all, and nobody would want to be loved out of a sense of obligation.

It is also worth mentioning that Rusty did nothing to earn the right to be adopted. Again, this mirrors our own adoption into God's family. It is the doctrine of grace, a difficult concept for the secular world to understand. This could be due to the fact that we are taught at a very young age that we can only obtain things like money, possessions, a slim figure, or even love through hard work. There is no "free lunch." There's always a catch. If something sounds too good to be true, then it probably is.

This mistrust of something offered freely is compounded by the wide range of scams and rip-offs that plague the internet. I'll never forget the time that Zach ordered a pair of socks from an online company. When they arrived, he was surprised to discover that they were child-sized!

Moreover, people feel a need to work for what they receive because they believe that in order for something to be valuable, it must be earned. Surely there must be a course to complete or a certain number of good deeds to be performed, right? Surely we must be deserving of eternal life for a reason that we can comprehend. Perhaps it is our lineage? All through the New Testament, groups of elite snobs touted their pedigree, their descent from Abraham, as a qualifier for their righteousness. This idea of "salvation by association" still exists in the minds of many people today. Suppose our parents or grandparents were good people. Wouldn't that merit us eternal life? According to scripture, we are each responsible for our own relationship with God. What if we attend church, preach, teach, sing, drive the church van, or help with Vacation Bible School? Our quid-pro-quo world would look at that resume and declare, *Yes, that person is surely heaven-bound.* However, the Bible refutes this idea of earned salvation.

Isaiah wrote in Isaiah 64:6 (KJV) that our righteousness is as "filthy rags." Jesus said in Matthew 7:22–23 that people will come to Him at the final judgment bragging about their works only to hear Him reply, "I never knew you; depart from me, you workers of lawlessness." The Apostle Paul wrote in Ephesians 2:8–9 that we are saved by grace through faith, not of works, so that no one can boast. God did all the heavy lifting in the work of our salvation at the cross. All that's required of us is to believe and receive.

However, there is one element of salvation that the secular world does understand in the matter of getting something for nothing. It's not what you know; it's whom you know. This fact of life often benefits us when we apply for a job or need a favor from someone in a position of power. It helps to have friends in high places, so having a relationship with Jesus is crucial to obtaining eternal life. The account of the thief on the cross as recorded in Luke 23:39–43 illustrates this simple truth:

> One of the criminals who were hanged railed at him, saying, "Are you not the Christ? Save yourself and us!" But the other rebuked him, saying, "Do you not fear God, since you are under the same sentence of condemnation? And we indeed justly, for we are receiving the due reward of our deeds; but this man has done nothing wrong." And he said, "Jesus, remember me when you come into your

kingdom." And he said to him, "Truly, I say to you, today you will be with me in paradise."

This guilty criminal never accomplished even one good work—except for this powerful testimony. He never served, tithed, attended one church service, or got baptized. (He would have done these things had he lived.) All this man did was recognize his sinful state, believe in Jesus as the Son of God, and, in faith, ask Him for salvation. As a result, Jesus promised him "paradise." He wasn't educated. He didn't know the scriptures, but he knew the one who wrote them was hanging on a cross beside him. It wasn't what he knew or did. It was whom he knew.

This begs the question of why.

Why would Jesus die for this man's sins and our sins as well when He knew that most of mankind would reject Him? The answer is simple yet profound: love. It is the same sort of love that a parent has for a child even before that child is born. We make the decision to have them, even though we know that they won't always return our love. They will rebel. They will make messes. They will scare us half to death. Still, we plow forth because our love for them outweighs everything else. Such was our affection for Rusty, of whose high maintenance we had been forewarned, and such is God's love for us (John 3:16). He looked ahead and saw every sin I would ever commit—all the tests that I would fail—yet He chose to save me anyway.

Lastly, like Rusty, we are given a new name.

Tina and I never really argued over naming the children. Zach and Jada aren't particularly trendy names. We simply liked the way that they sounded, and at the time of their births, we didn't know of any other babies with these names. Lately, it seems like every birth announcement includes a name that the parents simply invented in an attempt to surpass other parents in creativity and uniqueness. It's no wonder that nicknames eventually replace these monikers; hence, the ubiquity of the name Bubba.

This was not the case with biblical names. Those names had meaning. Sometimes the meaning was favorable, as with the name *Joshua,* which means "salvation is from the Lord," or *Samuel,* which means "God hears." Other times, the meaning of the name was actually unfavorable. For example, the name *Ichabod* means "the glory is gone."

Such names were not intended to be cruel. Instead, they usually reflected a feeling about a major event that took place at the time of birth. Names are apparently a big deal to God.

In Genesis 17:5, He changed Abram's name to Abraham because he would be a "father of a multitude of nations." God also changed the name of Abraham's wife from Sarai to Sarah, which in Hebrew means "princess." These are hardly names that we would associate with a couple who were ninety and a hundred years old, respectively, but God wasn't seeing their age or any other shortcomings. God saw their potential. The same thing happened to a fisherman named Simon in the New Testament. In John 1:42, Jesus changed his name to Peter, which means "rock."

Revelation 2:17 promises us each a new name in eternity.

This may be part of God's plan to make everything new, but for now, we get to bear the name Christian.

It's a reminder each time we hear it that we belong to Him now, and it also serves as an admonition to "walk in the same way in which He walked" (1 John 2:6). We also get to be called "children of God" as stated in John 1:12 as well as numerous other passages of scripture, and Galatians 4:6 tells us that in return, we can call Him "Abba! Father!" This is a term of closeness and endearment. It means that because He looked down and said, "I want Him," we get to have a personal relationship with the Creator of the universe, and all we have to do is receive Him by faith. Pretty cool, huh?

EVERYONE HATES CHANGE

We live in a world characterized by change. In fact, change is the only thing on earth that is truly consistent. The weather changes. The seasons change. Our bodies change. Leaders, laws, values, lifestyles, health, relationships, circumstances—they all change. As I've gotten older, I like to change less and less. However, God has used periods of change in my life to grow and shape me.

He removes me from my routines and comfort zones into places and circumstances that cause me to rely on Him, thereby increasing my faith. Even though I know that change is good for me, I fight it tooth and nail because, let's face it, change is tough.

As it turns out, change is also difficult for puppies, and I don't think that any of us were prepared for the changes that Rusty would bring into our lives. It all began the first night in his new home. After staying up late playing with our new friend, we were all very tired. After a quick walk in the backyard, we put Rusty in his crate with a bed, a puppy pad, and a little food and water.

"Good night, Rusty," we said as we closed the utility room door.

It was not a good night.

He began to protest loudly as soon as we shut the door. Tina and I exchanged worried looks.

"He'll settle down and go to sleep soon," she said, unsure that it was the truth.

The kids' bedrooms were on the opposite end of the house from our bedroom and the utility room, which now housed a loud, complaining dog. They were dreaming peacefully as we lay awake, listening to the crying. Then I remembered a trick I had learned while on a mission trip with my snoring older brothers. I dug through my night-stand drawer until I found my earplugs. They drowned out most of the noise, enabling me a little fitful slumber. I still woke up almost as tired as when I laid down.

"He. Has. Cried. All. Night," announced my cranky, bedraggled wife the next morning.

"Merry Christmas," I replied.

New sleep patterns weren't the only change. Just as we had suspected, puppy ownership was a lot of work. This involved feeding, bathing, walking, and cleaning up little "accidents" all over the house. As it turned out, Mrs. Maddox was correct in her assessment of Rusty's bowels. Immediately after eating, he and I would head to the backyard, where he would do his "business," and then he'd receive a treat. On one memorable, cold night, we went out for a walk and waited for what seemed like an eternity for him to pee. Finally, the mission was accomplished, and we went back inside, where Rusty, much to my chagrin, immediately drained his water bowl!

Eating a meal also changed for us as we discovered our puppy was a beggar. He would watch every bite that traveled from plate to mouth, and he was too cute to be refused at least a small morsel. (This would eventually lead to obesity and back problems, which required us to implement a diet.) In some ways, the life adjustments were similar to the ones we had made when we brought home our newborn babies, but this time, we had two extra pairs of hands to help. Both Zach and Jada assisted in the care of their new little brother. It was a labor of love because it wasn't just work. There was a lot of play involved to keep Rusty occupied and quiet.

The move must have been a huge adjustment for Rusty as well. Put yourself in his shoes. One minute, you're snoring contentedly with your littermates in your warm, safe little world, then suddenly, a loud, strange-smelling couple wraps you in a blanket, puts you in a cardboard box, and whisks you away from everything you've ever known and understood. You travel to an unfamiliar house and are greeted by two more strangers. These are loud, excitable creatures. You begin to shake nervously as they put you down on a soft carpet. They seem to want to play, and you oblige them. They roll some sort of round thing across the floor, and you chase it.

These creatures have no sharp teeth or claws, making it different from playing with your siblings, but it's fun nonetheless. Then you're taken outside, where the man puts you down on the cold ground. He seems to be waiting for something. You follow him around the yard, hoping he'll pick you up soon because it's freezing out here! All the walking makes you need to move your bowels. The man seems delighted, and he gives you something good to eat. *How strange*, you think as he picks you up and you go back inside. He wraps you in a blanket, puts you in a cage, turns off the light, and shuts the door. Where are the other puppies? Nope, this won't do. You yelp as loudly as you can for the remainder of the night. When they finally come to get you out of the cage the next morning, you smell good food on the stove. The kids seem excited again. There are colorful papers being torn, and new sights and sounds surround you. New clothes, books, video games, and other unidentifiable things are strewn all over the floor. *Do they do this every day?* You wonder.

"Merry Christmas, Rusty." (For some reason, they say that word when they talk to you.) One of them says as he tosses you a rawhide chew. Maybe this place isn't so bad after all.

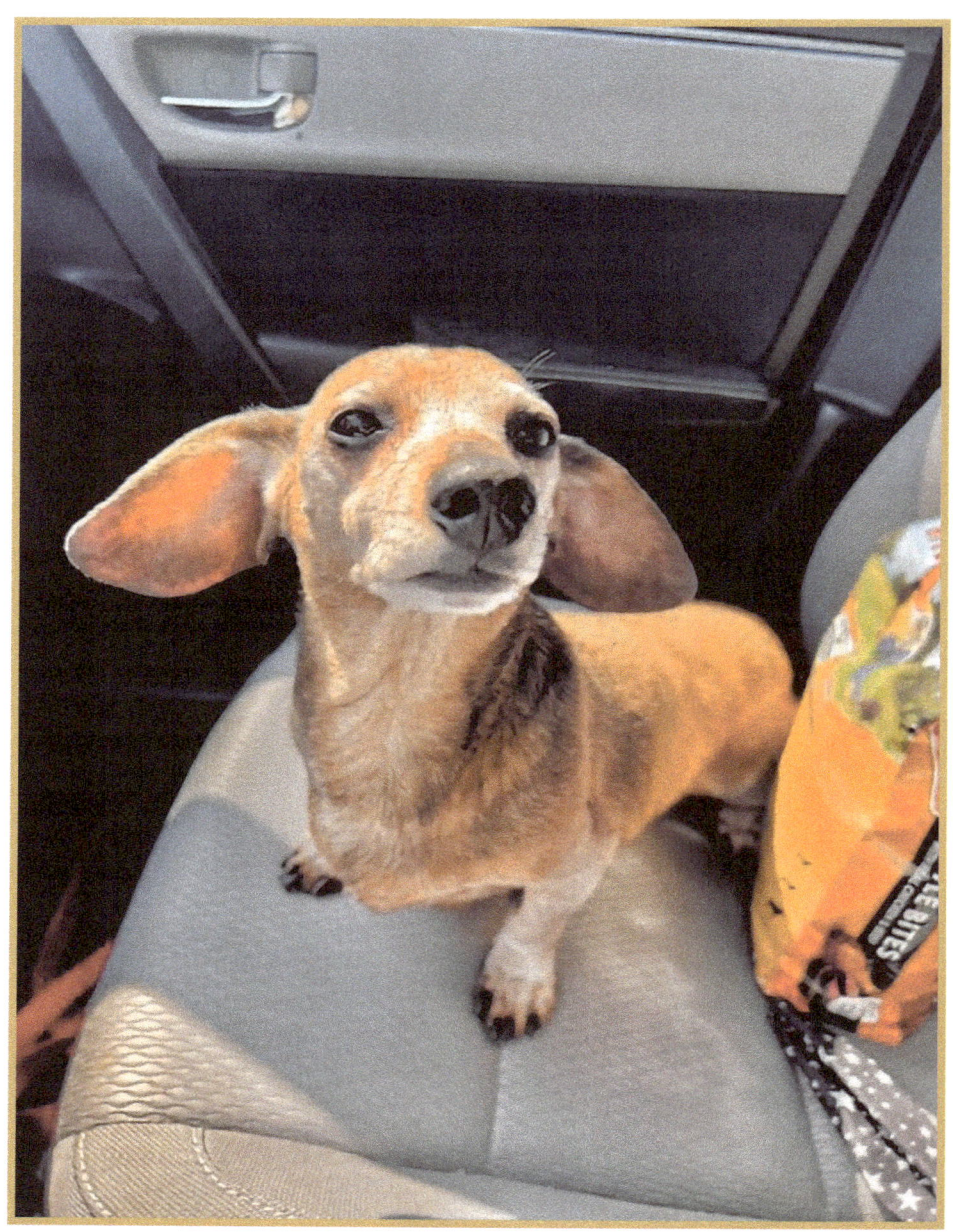

If Rusty had self-awareness, he would have seen his old life in very small terms. He lived in a small enclosure and interacted with very few people. His daily routine included eating, sleeping, and wrestling with his siblings. This was life—all of life—but he had no idea what was in store for him. After his adoption into the Hester family, his life became much larger. Suddenly, there were new, interesting foods to taste, aromas to sniff, and people to meet and play with. Instead of a small enclosure, he now had a whole house to roam in and a backyard to explore. There were rawhides to chew, snacks to steal, and cats to chase. Children visited from next door to run and play with him. What fun! His old life wouldn't have allowed him to even imagine these things. The same can be said for one newly adopted into the family of God.

> But as it is written, What no eye has seen, nor ear heard, nor the heart of man imagined, what God has prepared for those who love him. (1 Corinthians 2:9)

An unbeliever may envision Christian life as empty, a list of "thou shalt nots." They observe from a distance as a newly born-again child of God begins to change. This may look like turning over a new leaf or finally growing up, but it's much more than that.

> Therefore, if anyone is in Christ, he is a new creation. The old has passed away; behold, the new has come. (2 Corinthians 5:17)

It's a process called *sanctification*, where a believer grows ever closer to Jesus. His love and gratitude for his salvation inspire him to obey Christ, and as a result of this, he matures spiritually, sinning less and less. When he does sin, he feels a conviction in his heart that inspires him to repent, but that's only one aspect of the change in his heart and lifestyle. God gives much more than He takes. He gives us peace with Himself and the confidence to live life abundantly (John 14:27). He gives us the security of consistency and faithfulness in stark contrast to an ever-changing world (Hebrews 13:8). He gives us a sense of purpose that goes beyond making money and accomplishing our own goals (Mark 1:17). He replaces toxic relationships with brothers and sisters who love us and pray for us (John 15:12).

The Bible is full of people who thought they had life figured out. Their course, they thought, was set (just like Rusty). They were living a certain way, and for all they knew, they would die that way. Then Jesus changed their whole world.

Acts 3:1–10 tells us the story of a lame beggar, who sat every day by the temple gate. A daily routine of sitting and begging was his life—his entire life. That routine was turned on its ear one day when Peter and John walked by. Instead of giving him money, he healed him in the name of Jesus. The scripture says that he immediately began to walk, leap, and praise God. This was not the way he expected his day to end. We're not given any information about his life from that point on, but his options were wide open. Perhaps he learned a trade, started a family, or became a preacher. One thing's for sure: his begging days were over. In exchange for his old life of begging, God had graciously given him a new purpose. God always works that way. In fact, there isn't even one example of a person in the Bible—or since that time—who was saved, yet their life remained unchanged.

Sometimes lost folks see their lives in the same way the lame beggar saw his. They live by a routine: wake, eat, work, eat again, watch a little TV, sleep, and then do it all over. Somewhere in the backs of their minds, they know that there should be more to this existence, and they're right. In Ecclesiastes 3:11, Solomon wrote that God put eternity into our hearts. In the deepest reaches of their souls, people long to return to that perfect relationship with God that existed with Adam and Eve before sin entered the world. They recognize their need to change. They desire holiness and purity, but sadly, most of them will reject the only source of those things, attempting to achieve them in their own ways. The only way to true righteousness is to allow God to adopt you and change you, and that requires faith. Abram was a man who learned a lot about faith and change. Genesis 12 tells us God called Abraham—at age seventy-five—to leave his homeland for a place that He would show him.

Can you imagine that? Abram left without knowing where he was going! He was satisfied by the fact that God knew his destination and that faith would sustain him for the rest of his days. Of course, he would have seasons of doubt. He would sin as we all do (Romans 3:23). Some of his sins would have far-reaching consequences that are still felt today, but by and large, he trusted God. This allowed him to experience change without despair and to live by faith in what I call the *in-between*.

> By faith Abraham, when he was called, obeyed and set out for a place that he was going to receive as an inheritance. He went out, even though he did not know where he was going. By faith he stayed as a foreigner in the land of promise, living in tents as did Isaac and Jacob, coheirs of the same promise. For he was looking forward to the city that has foundations, whose architect and builder is God. (Hebrews 11:8–10 CSB)

One of the most amazing aspects of this passage is about living in tents. When living a nomadic lifestyle, one is never in a stable, secure place. You're in a constant period of transition, and that can be intense (pun intended). Life is full of transition periods. A new job is hectic at first, but eventually, you become accustomed to the new hours, responsibilities, and coworkers. A marriage is also a huge change. Instead of parting at the end of an evening, you both retire to the same bed. You eat, bathe, cook, clean, entertain, pay bills, and watch television together. Then, as you get used to that lifestyle, you decide to start a family.

Again, life is thrown into chaos.

Your world suddenly revolves around diapers, formula, baby clothes, and pediatrician visits. Then comes their childhood and more changes. After that comes adolescence and changes. Then, just when things have seemed to settle into some sort of normalcy, they move out, and you're left with just your spouse.

This cycle of changing and settling is similar to a child's game of musical chairs. You're walking. The music is playing. The suspense builds. Where will you land? In this game or in the game of life, it's imperative that we walk by faith, just like Abraham, Isaac, and Jacob, trusting in the One who never changes. We don't have to know where we'll land. He knows, and that's enough.

The other aspect of change involves another Rusty story. It's a tale called "Clawstrimphobia."

We had dogs in the family home where I was raised. They were never purebred (except for one bird dog). They never lived to old age (except for that same bird dog), and I never remember trimming their toenails as these were rugged outdoor mutts. Their nails wore down naturally as a result of their activity.

I was surprised to realize that Rusty, whose domain was largely carpet and soft grass, would need his nails cut as a part of his regular grooming. This was complicated by the fact that he suffered from that phobia. This is a fear commonly held by spoiled brat, prima donna dachshunds. Oh, the drama!

There was whining, crying, barking, snarling, and growling involved, and that was just to determine who would take him to the veterinarian's office. (They're cheaper than the groomer.)

The unlucky soul (usually me) who lost this battle would first retrieve the harness and leash from the pantry, as Rusty would need a walk before getting into a vehicle. Upon seeing the leash, he would immediately stop whatever he was doing and run to a hiding spot between Tina's chair and the end table. It wasn't that we couldn't see him there, but it was an aggravation to drag him out. He hated the harness, but rather than fight the inevitable, he would go as limp as a dishrag, like a toddler torn from a playground. After suffering the walk around our block and being loaded into the vehicle, Rusty would ride in sulky silence for the entire trip. You'd find a happier disposition in a death row inmate walking their last mile.

He had to be carried into the vet's office. The vet assistant pulled his folder, which contained Rusty's medical records and vaccination history. I noticed the word *screamer* written in Sharpie on the first page. This particular assistant had never cut his nails, so I warned her about his "clawstrimphobia."

"You're gonna need a muzzle and some help," I cautioned.

It was all I could do to hold onto him as she retrieved those. He was in full panic mode now because he knew what was coming. His little heart was a jackhammer in his chest, and his eyes widened in fear. Putting him on the exam table was out of the question, as he would surely have plunged off in a *Thelma & Louise* nosedive. The assistant applied the muzzle and began. One held the dog, while the other managed the clippers. He was tolerant of the first few nails on his front feet, but then he began to struggle and twist. It was all they could do to hold him as they attempted to calm him with stroking and soft words. He wanted none of it and looked at me pleadingly, *Can't we go home? Why are you letting them do this to me?* His eyes seem to say.

The dew claws turned out to be a little tricky as they had already begun to curl. The back feet were worse for some reason, and he resumed his struggles. Inevitably, they would cut at least one into the quick, and Rusty began to twist and thrash in a way that reminded me of the Tasmanian Devil. He was slobbering and whining, madder than a mashed cat. I could only imagine what the people in the waiting room were thinking.

Once it was over, a medicinal powder was applied to the nails, which were cut too short. They removed the muzzle and offered him a treat, which he rudely declined. I put him down so that I could pay the bill, and he made a beeline for the door: *Now can we go?*

"You weren't very well-behaved," I chided as I loaded him into the car. I imagine that if he had possessed the necessary dexterity, he would've given me the finger. Instead, he snorted in derision. He was calm, even to the point of dozing (or pouting) on the trip home, but as we entered our neighborhood, he excitedly jumped into my lap, awash with relief. It was over until next time.

This may have seemed cruel to him, and he surely wondered why he had to endure it. He doesn't understand the potential problems that would arise as a result of not trimming his nails. He doesn't know that they would eventually curl under and cut into the pads of his feet. He doesn't realize that walking would become more difficult than impossible. All that he can see is the pain, resentment, fear, and inconvenience of the present moment.

Any maturing Christian can relate to Rusty. None of us like to be "pruned," yet that is exactly what Jesus promises will happen to us: "I am the true vine, and my Father is the vinedresser. Every branch in me that does not bear fruit he takes away, and every branch that does bear fruit he prunes, that it may bear more fruit" (John 15:1–2).

This can be a difficult change for new believers, yet without this pruning, we never reach our potential as followers of Christ. Unpruned, we will be only spectators watching from the sidelines as others perform the ministries that God had intended for us to do. Just as Rusty's toenails slowly yet surely grow, so will we grow in apathy, discontentment, bitterness, and unhappiness. Just as Rusty would be hindered in his ability to walk, so, too, would our spiritual walk be hampered by unpruned sin (Hebrews 12:1). The unpruned Christian will usually become critical of those serving God, and they will usually say things like, "I didn't get anything out of that service," forgetting that the service is about worshipping God—not entertainment. They will also become critical of the people who are actually doing something in the church in an attempt to take the spotlight off of their own laziness.

When we find ourselves in this mindset, we are in desperate need of good pruning. We need to confess our sin and repent of it, placing our faith in God for the power to defeat it. Just as Rusty can't trim his own nails, we can't prune the sin out of our own lives. We must allow the Gardener/Groomer to do His job. It can be messy and painful, and like Rusty, we usually resist. Unlike Rusty, we must allow it to happen, as God still allows us free will.

The pruning process will look different in the life of each new or rededicated believer because we're all different. We all have that one branch (sin) that we want to keep. We feed and water it, making it stronger and more difficult to relinquish. For instance, the person who has a problem with lust feeds that sin with things like pornography and a wandering eye. The gossiper will feed that sin in the company of other gossipers. The one who uses foul language will feed that sin with entertainment choices (books, movies, etc.) that include profanity. God wants to remove all of these from the hearts of His children. Like any good parent, He loves us too much to let us run wild. However, there doesn't seem to be any sort of order to the pruning process. He may first convict one person's heart concerning honesty, while a different person is first convicted of drunkenness, etc.

With this in mind, we shouldn't judge one another concerning the sin in our lives, nor can we prune away someone else's sin. Leave that task to the Gardener because He is the only one qualified for the job. He works in His own way and in His own timing but make no mistake. Pruning will happen so that we can bear fruit. This fruit includes the works we do, the people to whom we bear witness, and a heart that increasingly reflects the heart of Jesus. Some of the characteristics of such a heart are listed in Galatians

5:22–23. They are love, joy, peace, patience, kindness, goodness, faithfulness, gentleness, and self-control.

We want this "fruit" in our lives, but it requires change and often sacrifice. For example, Mark 1:18 tells us that when Jesus called Simon and Andrew to follow Him, they immediately left their fishing nets to do so. Luke 5:27–28 tells us Jesus called a tax collector named Levi to follow Him, and Levi (also known as Matthew) obeyed, abandoning his collection booth. Some are called to the mission field. Some are called to preach. Another might be called to simply walk across a room and share his testimony with someone who is lost. The sacrifice may mean giving up a relationship, habit, or lifestyle that is in conflict with scripture. It will be awkward and painful, requiring us to exercise faith. Anyone who has ever followed Christ into the unknown will attest to this, but they will also tell you that the rewards of obedience far outweigh the suffering. It also becomes a powerful part of our testimony, which will glorify the One who never changes. Don't worry. God holds the clippers, so let Him do His work.

GOD SPELLED
BACKWARD IS DOG

Okay, I'll admit it. I've never sat down and written out a budget. (Somewhere, Dave Ramsey just gasped and clutched his chest.) I fully realize that all households, businesses, churches, and governments operate most efficiently when they make and adhere to a budget. After all, there is only a limited amount of capital to spend on the things we want or need, so we must carefully consider whether we can afford a luxury item before we make a purchase. This means that we need to prioritize our needs over our wants. Thus, we make wise decisions with our incomes.

At least, that's the way it's supposed to work. In reality, households overspend and necessities are sacrificed for the sake of luxuries. Credit cards max out. People default on loans. Cars get repossessed. Businesses make the same types of mistakes, but on a larger scale, when they invest poorly in new ventures or hire unqualified people. It's no wonder that so many start-ups fail. Even churches are susceptible to poor budgeting, making decisions based on man-made plans rather than God's design. They hire or spend unwisely, and important ministries and charities suffer as a result. Governments attempt to disguise poor budgeting by simply printing more money, and while it is possible to create more money, it's impossible to create actual wealth. Their spending habits remind me of a close relative of mine who, upon losing his job, purchased a new outboard motor for his boat. When someone questioned him about the timing of his new acquisition, he replied, "When I had a job, I didn't really need a boat." I'm happy to report that he learned from his mistakes and has become a successful entrepreneur (with a much nicer boat), but he never would have done so without learning to prioritize.

I've learned that money isn't the only thing I need to prioritize. They print more cash every day, but things like time and energy are finite. These must be weighed and allotted carefully to each aspect of life with great care. Sometimes, God tests us to show us exactly how we have prioritized time, energy, and money. Once again, He used

Rusty on a typical school morning to teach me this lesson. In all honesty, these events didn't all take place on one specific morning; rather, the following morning was an amalgamation of mornings during my children's teenage years. Almost all parents will catch a glimpse of themselves here.

The morning begins with a small, almost imperceptible whine. I look at the clock, which reads 4:30. If he goes away, I can sleep for another half hour, yet the whining increases in both tone and volume. It is now accompanied by toenails dancing on a hardwood floor. Rusty cannot enter our carpeted bedroom, but he will not cease the whining that has grown into a low growl. Still, I hope against hope that he will relent, although at this point I'm wide awake. Then, with his patience at an end, my dog produces an ear-splitting sound unduplicated in the animal kingdom. Perhaps this is what Walt Whitman had in mind when he wrote of a "barbaric yawp." It's a combination of a yawn, whine, and bark. Imagine a cross between a wookie's growl and a velociraptor's shriek.

Defeated, I get up to let him out, but as it turns out, I'm too late. There is a mess to clean, and even as I tackle this job, Rusty continues to frolic at my feet. His wagging tail is a blur, and his ears are raised. He speaks not in words but in actions that convey his desires. *Hey, Dad, look at me. Pet me. Pick me up. Can I have my breakfast now?*

I ignore him and proceed with the morning routine of making coffee and packing my lunch. I glance at my Bible lying atop a barstool next to the kitchen counter, but just as I am about to pick it up, I realize that it is Friday. I haven't studied my Sunday school lesson yet. I give it a quick read and recognize the scripture passage. This should be an easy one as the verses are familiar. After jotting down a few quick notes, I get on with my morning. After I shower, shave, and dress, the rest of the household begins to stir. Rusty didn't want me to leave him alone in the living room and woke them all with more barking and whining: *Doesn't anyone realize that I haven't been fed yet? WAKE UP, PEOPLE!*

The kids need attention with clothes, shoes, lunches, and "oh yeahs."

"Oh yeah," my firstborn chirps. "I need twenty dollars for—." This school expense could be almost anything, and it's usually something I assumed was already covered on April 15.

Of course, I'm broke, so I employ that time-tested reply of all dads everywhere.

"Go ask your mother." Meanwhile, Rusty has resumed his dance, which is now punctuated with an occasional spin and roll over.

Good morning, Zach! Feed me. Pet me. Look at me. Talk to me.

My younger child also needs attention.

"Oh yeah," she chimes. "I almost forgot. You know how this is spirit week at school?" (To be honest, I hadn't really given it much thought.) "Well, I need to dress like a nerd today, so do you have a shirt I can borrow?"

"Let me get this straight," I reply somewhat wounded. "You need to dress like a nerd, and you think that my clothing will help you accomplish this goal?"

Good morning, Jada. Pet me. Talk to me. Play with me. Feed me!

"Sure," she replies innocently. "I need a plaid shirt with a button-down collar. Do you have one?"

"Yes," I reply sheepishly as I turn to go fetch it for her. "Do you want the usual for lunch?" (This is macaroni and cheese from a single-serve pouch prepared in the micro-wave and packed into a hot food container.)

"Yes, but don't use all the cheese in the package."

"Because?"

"It'll be too cheesy."

It's a good thing she's cute.

That smells good. Can I have a bite? Look at me. I'm still waiting down here.

I realize as I pick up my lunch, coffee, and keys that I've neglected the little guy for most of the morning, but work, family, ministry, food, clothing, and life in general have taken precedence over my quality time with Rusty. I'll pay him some attention when I get home.

"Be a good puppy, Rusty," I say as I dump some food in his bowl and head out the door.

It's about time.

I am a mailman, or a letter carrier if you prefer the politically correct terminology, so the Christmas season is the most hectic time of the year. Work is a bear. We're shorthanded, so five people must do the work of six. I get the lion's share as I am the newest employee, and I'm still trying to impress the management. Customers are crabby. Traffic is a nightmare. The mail and package volume is twice the normal level, and there is a circular mailing.

(Every box on the route gets one.) My breathing becomes labored several times, and I realize that my anxiety level is rising. Finally, the workday ends, and nothing has ever felt so good as clocking out. Still, there is work waiting for me at home in the form of mowing, laundry, and assisting with homework that I don't understand. (What happened to math?) All the while, Rusty follows me excitedly in a vain attempt to get me to play.

Hey, Dad! You're home! Look at me. Talk to me. Pet me. Play with me.

He carries a ball in his mouth in the hope that I will throw it for him. After which, he will chase it, attack it, and bring it back, but he won't actually give it to me. Instead, he will put it under the couch, where he will bark at it until someone fetches it for him! This game could go on for an eternity, and it requires more energy than I am willing or able to spend.

"Not now," I tell him as I finally sit down to enjoy a hot meal. He sits at my feet and looks up at me expectantly, waiting for crumbs to fall like the Israelites waiting for manna from heaven. (This may sound like an aggravation, but it actually saves us a lot of sweeping.) He knows that the real prize is that last bite, and he waits for it patiently with just a little drooling. He has learned that if I have eaten my fill and if I'm feeling generous, I will allow him that last morsel.

Wow! That smells good. Can I have a bite?

"Here you go," I say as I drop a small hunk of bread crust. I watch as he gobbles it, and I congratulate myself on being a good dog dad. Most days, I really am a good pet owner. I give Rusty lots of time, attention, energy, and snacks, but it's all done on my schedule. I am the one in control of this relationship, and while he is an important part of my life, he isn't my whole life. After all, he's just a dog.

Is it any wonder that God and dog have opposite spellings? Whether we realize it or not, we often prioritize other things ahead of Him. These aren't necessarily what most of us would consider bad. The list includes family, work, hobbies, ministries, and necessities, and all of these have a place in my life. They become problematic when I allow them to take the place of my personal relationship with God. When I do this, I am treating God like a dog.

I ignored Rusty. He wanted communication and attention, but I blew him off for other things that I considered to be of more importance. When I neglect to begin the day with prayer and Bible study, I am treating God like my dog, and I am denying myself what I need the most—time alone with God. 1 Samuel 12:23 tells us that ceasing to pray is a sin. Ephesians 6:18 tells us to pray at all times in the Spirit. 1 Thessalonians 5:17 tells us to pray constantly. James 5:13 reminds us to pray for the people who are suffering. Philippians 4:6 tells us to bring our requests to God and then to be at peace about whatever it is that we prayed for. Jesus taught His disciples to pray in Matthew 6:9–13 (the Lord's prayer), and He also took time to withdraw from the world and pray alone, as is recorded in Matthew 14:23. His example serves to remind us that communication is vital to our relationship with God. If He needed that time alone with the Father, then so do we. Imagine how much better I would have reacted to the difficult day if I had begun it with prayer.

I was too tired to play with Rusty. When we fail to give God the first and best of our energy, we are treating Him like a dog. We have a limited amount of energy each day, and with age comes the realization that our energy levels are much lower than they used to be. Therefore, we must budget it more carefully. Too often, we allow other things to sap our energy stores, and the works to which He has called us suffer from neglect. Maybe there was someone on my route who needed me to stop and pray for them. Maybe I was supposed to encourage them. Maybe there was even someone in my path that day who needed to hear the gospel.

Ephesians 2:10 tells us that God sets up good works for us to do. The problem is that we are often too busy or preoccupied to take notice of them. God deserves better than that. He is not content to be only a part of our lives, but when we worship Him only on Sundays or when we pray only before a meal (habitually, as if on autopilot), then that is exactly where we have placed Him in our energy budget. Instead of God being just one part of our lives, He desires our lives to be part of His plan. The Apostle Paul explained it best in Galatians 2:20: "I have been crucified with Christ. It is no longer I who live, but Christ who lives in me. And the life I now live in the flesh I live by faith in the Son of God, who loved me and gave himself for me."

I gave Rusty the last leftover bite of my meal. When we give God our unwanted leftovers, we are treating Him like a dog. These leftovers are not only communication, time, and energy, but also (gasp) money. Money can be a touchy subject. Maybe that's because of the dishonest televangelists (although certainly not all televangelists) who constantly promise prosperity and blessings in exchange for your donations. Sermons about tithing are rare nowadays, and that's a shame as Jesus had plenty to say about the subject of money. In fact, the Bible is a wealth (pardon the pun) of information about what we should give and why we should give it.

2 Corinthians 9:7 tells us that we are to give cheerfully. This can be difficult in a culture that seems to see money as lifeblood, especially for those of us who grew up in the seventies and eighties. We are conditioned, at an early age, to ask ourselves if we make enough or have saved enough, so in order to give our money cheerfully, we must begin— as a result of our new birth—to see it the way God sees it. Jesus pointed out the fact that treasures on earth are subject to time, theft, and decay, while treasures in heaven are eternal and therefore the wiser investment (Matthew 6:19–21).

Adoption of this mindset concerning money (or anything else for that matter) requires faith because treasure on earth can be seen and touched, whereas treasure in heaven is unseen in the here and now. The cheerful giver gives as a result of this faith, trusting in God to use the offering for kingdom growth. After all, nobody wants to give money to someone they don't trust. Furthermore, the cheerful giver will view giving as an act of worship, just like singing, testifying, or serving. He will not give in order to attempt to gain favor with God, as he understands that God doesn't really need his money. Rather, he will see that he needs to give it, and he knows that giving it is a privilege, not a burden. A faith-based attitude is what God really desires in our giving. This probably explains why Abel's gift was accepted and Cain's was not (Genesis 4:3–5).

Finally, giving should be sacrificial. Too often, we give our leftover money to God in much the same manner as I give my leftovers to my dog. That isn't really a sacrifice. In Malachi 1:8, God uses His prophet to chastise the priests of that time for offering blind, lame, or otherwise unwanted animals on the altar. Their attitudes toward giving seemed to be marked by a sense of apathy. "Tired of caring for that sick animal? Bring it down to the temple, and we'll throw it on the altar. Problem solved." He points to the fact that they wouldn't dare to treat their governor that way, so why would they treat God that way? Their attitude was revealed by their actions. This sort of offering shows no gratitude, love, or respect from the offerer. Malachi 1:10 tells us that God neither wants nor accepts that kind of offering.

Instead, we should follow the example of the widow in Luke 21:2–4. Other people were giving out of their abundance, while she gave only two small coins, all that she had. Jesus remarked that she had given more than anyone else. When I read about people like that, I have to stop and examine my own life. Where does the bulk of my time, attention, energy, and money go? What am I giving, and why am I giving it? Everyone actually budgets for these things, whether they admit it to themselves or not.

What happens when we don't give God the place that He deserves our priority budget? He will awaken our attention in a way that is similar to the way that Rusty awakened me. It will begin with a still, small voice. Maybe we read some scripture; we hear a song or sermon; we get a word from a

Christian friend. The Holy Spirit uses this to tell us what we need to change or do. If we fail to act on this word from God, He will speak louder. We may find that our prayers seem hindered. We may even lose sleep. There will be a nagging sense of something being wrong or undone. If we still refuse to listen, God will force us from our spiritual slumber with a "barbaric yawp." This yawp will usually take the form of a difficult situation that causes us to cry out to God for relief.

Examine the book of Jonah. God instructed Jonah to go and preach a sermon to a wicked city, but instead of following in obedience, he ignored the still, small voice. He boarded a ship that was headed in the opposite direction, so God spoke louder in the form of a storm that threatened to sink the ship. Jonah knew that this was God's work, and he could have simply told the sailors to turn back to their point of origin. Instead, he told them to throw him into the sea. They complied, and immediately, the storm ceased. It was at this point that God issued His "barbaric yawp" in the form of a giant fish that He had prepared for just this moment. It swallowed Jonah and kept him in its belly for three days. Finally, Jonah repented of his disobedience, and the fish spit him out onto dry land. God repeated his original instructions, and this time, Jonah obeyed.

I can't really sit in judgment of Jonah. Sometimes I push my luck even to the point of needing to hear a yawp. The Bible is full of such stories to remind us that God comes first, so let's give Him His rightful place in our budgets. He's not a dog.

THE RAISIN BRAN INCIDENT

I had wanted a black and tan dachshund, thinking of their facial markings as cute little bandit masks, but I was out-voted by my wife, who preferred the rusty-red puppies. As it turns out, not all bandits wear masks. This was proven by our own puppy, who turned out to be a thief comparable to Bilbo Baggins and a vandal who rivaled a New York train graffiti artist. He wasn't malicious, but he was quite mis-chievous in his activities, especially in regard to the garbage can. Its aroma must have been irresistible, because as soon as he possessed the strength, weight, and height to topple it, down it came—a cornucopia of foul-smelling wrappers and morsels of food. At this point, we would hurry into the kitchen and scold him, sending him out while we cleaned up his mess and robbing him of his ill-gotten spoils.

Dogs are like any other animals that act on instinct, so I won't claim that he was lacking in moral fiber or conscience. He knew neither, yet he was intelligent enough to learn when he could get away with trash can destruction and when he could not. This sense of prudence soon led him to only tip over the garbage while we were not home, and who wants to come home from a hard day's work only to have to attempt to remove coffee grounds from the carpet?

My initial solution was to cleverly chain the can to the wall, thus making it immovable. Rusty responded by removing the lid and dragging the bag out. Next, we decided to store the can in one of the cabinets and were awestruck to discover that Rusty—who lacks opposable thumbs—was capable of opening a cabinet door! He even upped his game by attacking not only the garbage but also our groceries. These he raided in a way that would have impressed a Viking. His list of victims included crackers, instant oatmeal, cereal, pasta, and anything else that caught his eye. He ate it all, leaving chewed wrappers and packaging strewn in his wake like battlefield carnage.

That is how, even though our kids were out of the baby stage, we wound up with childproof locks on our cabinets. Our Facebook friends found this quite amusing when Tina shared a picture of our anti-theft system, but we were will-ing to endure a little teasing if it meant no more "clean up on aisle five" situations.

The funny thing about locks is that they only work when you remember to engage them, and every time we left the house without making sure to check the locks, we came home to a mess. At this point, Tina would once again take a picture of the damage to post it on Facebook, where our friends would comment things like, "Rusty strikes again." One such lapse in our diligence turned out to have disastrous repercussions.

It was a Saturday night that had capped off a long week. Work, school, and other various activities had left us all drained, so we decided to treat ourselves to a relaxing evening of shopping as well as supper at a nice restaurant. As a result, our spirits were somewhat buoyed and refreshed as we pulled into the driveway. However, our good mood would not last long.

As we approached the front door, we felt a palpable sense of dread and foreboding because Rusty did not run to the front door to greet us. Instead, he ran to the back door to be let out. It was not unlike Adam and Eve attempting to hide from God after they had so obviously sinned.

"Oh no," Tina moaned as she turned the corner and caught sight of our violated kitchen and living room. "RUSTY!"

Sure enough, we had neglected to lock the cabinets, and we beheld the consequences of our mistake. Rusty's tastes must have become more evolved and refined because he had passed on the garbage and gone straight for the goodies! He chewed into several sleeves of crackers (both round and graham), opened a box of instant oatmeal packets, and covered them in teeth marks and slobber; even a package of whole wheat pasta had fallen victim to his assault. However, none of these would have had the monumental outcome of his biggest crime.

We looked, horrified, at a disemboweled box of raisin bran.

Raisins can cause kidney failure in dogs, but at the time of this incident, I was only focused on the immediate effects of the bran on his digestive system. We allowed him to stay outside for a while in hopes that it would quickly leave his stomach, but none of us were that lucky as we were in for a long night.

The bran flakes began to attack his belly sometime around 9:00 p.m., my usual bedtime. He was uncomfortable to the point of misery, and sleep was out of the question (for all of us). He would settle for a few minutes, then we'd hear the scurrying of toenails across the floor. We nicknamed this sound "poop run," signaling the beginning of a race to the back door before it was, well, too late. Finally, after several such sprints, he seemed to fall into a fitful slumber, so we followed suit. Just as I began to doze off, I heard him whine from the other side of the baby gate that separated our bedroom entrance from the adjoining room. I quickly staggered out of bed, still half asleep and stumbling in the dark, and just as I put my bare foot down on the other side of the gate, I realized that I had been too slow. I immediately—and I'm sorry to say—loudly identified the substance into which I'd stepped. It wasn't one of my finest moments.

In retrospect, I can see that God can use any situation as a teaching tool because I learned some lessons from that experience.

The first thing I learned is that what goes into us dictates what affects us on the inside and also determines what comes out. Rusty had chosen to fill himself with things that he knew we had forbidden. We didn't attempt to place this limitation on him because we were mean. On the contrary, we forbade only the things that we knew would harm him. The same holds true for God. Maybe we can't always understand the harm in what God defines as sin, but we must trust Him to know what's best for us. It's not unlike when we tell our children, "Because I said so."

This presents us with a couple of questions: What are the things I should put into my mind, and how do I put them there? Think of the heart as an empty vessel that we fill with something every day. We fill it in a variety of ways, the most obvious of which is our choice of entertainment. We pick up our phones. We turn on our televisions. We use our computers. All of these grant us instant access to what we want to see and hear. According to Philippians 4, we are to think of things that are honorable, just, pure, lovely, commendable, excellent, or worthy of praise. Of course, what we think about is dependent wholly on the images and sounds we put into our eyes, ears, and hearts. These things can hurt us or they can help us. We must allow God's word to help us choose what is best for us as well as what glorifies Him.

For example, Jesus warned us in Matthew 5:28 that looking lustfully at a woman results in the same amount of guilt as actually committing adultery with her. In the old days, anyone who wanted pornography had to go out and buy it. Nowadays, it's only a mouse-click away, and these images don't just download to our hard drives. They are also imprinted on our hearts. This sin comes back to us in the way we view members of the opposite sex. We begin to see them as objects of desire rather than as souls for whom Jesus died. We add or subtract their value based on their looks. This comes with a hefty dose of guilt as well as a strained relationship with God.

The same holds true for the type of language that we use. It is the direct result of the language that we hear. Most parents have at least one story of their two-year-old repeating something that they should never have heard. The reason that I cursed that night was mostly due to the type of movies, television, and reading materials I had been ingesting. What went in came right back out, and I'm sorry to say that this wasn't an isolated incident. I've even done it in front of unbelievers, and in doing so, I damaged my witness to them. Colossians 3:8–9 (CSB) warns us about anger, rage, malice, slander, filthy language, and lying. These aren't just available in the entertainment choices we make. They also influence us through the company we keep. In short, if your friends have foul mouths, it is likely that you'll add certain words to your vocabulary. In 1 Corinthians 15:33, Paul writes that bad company corrupts good character. The good news is that it also works in the opposite way. Our language can be positively influenced by associating with other Christians. (Sunday school starts at 9:30.)

Of course, we must also live and work in a sin-filled world. We can't lock ourselves away in a tower somewhere, so we must learn to set boundaries with the unsaved people in our lives. When we do join in or approve of the sinning, we are conforming to the world—exactly what we are instructed not to do in Romans 12:1–2. Conforming to the world ruins our witness. We also distance ourselves from God, who is too holy to be in the presence of sin. Lastly, we become unhappy as the conviction from God's Holy Spirit robs us of our peace until we repent. Rusty proved it. What comes out is an awful mess.

Daniel was a good example of a man who knew how to set boundaries. He was removed from his home as a teenager as a result of the Babylonian invasion. Having been taken to King Nebuchadnezzar as a spoil of war, he was forced to change everything familiar to him. His language, wardrobe, education, and even name had to conform to the Babylonian lifestyle, but he drew the line at changing his kosher diet (Daniel 1:8). He also refused to stop praying (Daniel 6:10). He knew that such compromises would displease God. Such was his influence on his friends Shadrach, Meshach, and Abednego that they refused to worship an idol even when they were threatened with death. What had gone into Daniel, a godly upbringing, came right back out and was demonstrated in his refusal to conform to the sin that surrounded him.

Fast forward to the New Testament to see an even better (of course) example of someone who knew how to live in a sin-sick world without conforming to it. Jesus was criticized by the religious leaders of his time because He associated with known sinners. He was unfazed by this criticism because He had come for the sick, not the well (Matthew 9:12–13). However, we never see even one instance in which He approved or joined them in sinning.

The second lesson I learned from the raisin bran incident involves walking in darkness. I had been so focused on saving our living room carpet that I had neglected to turn on a light, and my poor, unprotected foot had paid the price. The Bible teaches us a lot about walking in darkness in a spiritual sense, and it usually associates darkness with danger, sin, and godlessness. These were the dangers of which David wrote in Psalm 23, when he had to walk through the valley of the shadow of death. Throughout much of his life, David was on the run from people who wanted to kill him. In order to deal with these trials, he clung closely to God, who was his only source of hope and light. Jesus described, in several of His parables, eternal separation from God's presence as being cast out into darkness. In fact, one of the first things that God created was light (Genesis 1:3). When we are redeemed at the end of time, there will be no more night (Revelation 22:5). In between these times, we must choose to walk either in darkness or in light.

Jesus is described by John as the light that shines in darkness (John 1:5). He shone the way to peace with God. His light cut through the darkness of legalism and the false teachings of the religious leaders of that day, who hated Him and rejected the grace through faith that He offered. They were motivated by jealousy and not by a desire for righteousness. Their actions (fruit) proved this. John went on to explain that people like that actually prefer the darkness of their own theologies and opinions to the light of the gospel of truth that was and still is offered through faith in Christ. Light exposes the things that darkness hides. They wanted to continue to hide their greed, self-centeredness, and lies under a facade of holiness. It's no wonder that Jesus called them whitewashed tombs, which were lovely on the outside but inside contained dead men's bones.

Shame on them, right? Usually, when I read about people in the Bible who've really messed up, I see the need to examine my own heart. I find it necessary to question my own motives for the work I do. Am I doing them for the sake of my own reputation and the applause of others, or because I love God and want to obey Him? Does my Monday through Friday life match my Sunday morning testimony? If not, then I need to repent because I've become just as much a "whitewashed" tomb as they were.

Nobody just wakes up one morning and decides to become a hypocrite like that. It's a mindset that creeps up on us unnoticed as a result of neglecting to spend time with God. We skip prayer time. We skip Bible study. We find ourselves serving the church rather than serving God. These red flags indicate a need to go back to the beginning of our relationship with Him, not for salvation but for a fresh start. We are promised this fresh start in 1 John 1:9: "If we confess our sins, he is faithful and just to forgive us our sins and to cleanse us from all unrighteousness."

In fact, the book of 1 John gives us even more details about the metaphor of either walking in light or in darkness. For starters, we must acknowledge the fact that everyone, even believers, sins. This is stated clearly in 1 John 1:8. However, we see that the believer is not content to walk in darkness, as described in 1:6. Think of it this way: when I stepped in that steamy pile on that fateful night, I immediately took my foot out of it, and I didn't want to take another step without first getting clean and turning on a light. The same holds true for the child of God who sins. God's Holy Spirit will let him know that what he is doing is wrong and that he needs to repent. His love for God will be evident in his changed walk. Such is not the case with the false prophet or teacher. Not only will he be content to walk in darkness, He will claim that what he stepped in was in fact a pile of daisies. Not only that. He will spread it with him wherever he walks. With this in mind, we need to be careful of those to whom we listen, but how do we identify someone who walks in darkness?

In 1 John, God provides us with a list of red flags that help us spot a false teacher walking in darkness: They will make false claims of fellowship with God (1:6). These are the casual "Christians" who want to be seen in church, but they don't reflect the fruit of the Spirit in any other way during the rest of the week. They will not give sacrificially, nor will they hold up under persecution.

The dark walker will be disobedient to God's commands (2:4). A saving relationship with Jesus means that He is not only the atoning sacrifice; He is also the Lord. Furthermore, Jesus told His disciples that if they loved Him, they would follow His commands. That applies to both the things we should do as well as the things we should not do, so when we disobey God, we are displaying both a lack of respect as well as a lack of love.

Additionally, this false teacher will hate their brother or sister (2:9). While it's natural to hate an enemy and love a friend, Jesus called on us to love the enemy also, and He admonished His followers to love their enemies in ways that even included feeding and clothing them. This supernatural way of loving is possible only with the enabling of God's Holy Spirit (who is absent in the life of the false prophet). John explains (5:3) that this love is a command. Therefore, it is not merely a suggestion.

The one who walks in darkness will love worldly things (2:15), and in our culture, there is a plethora of stuff to love. Advertisers and peers attempt to make us feel inferior if we don't have the latest model of phone or automobile. The love of money will drive us to multiple sins, and we begin to love what can be seen and touched rather than God, whom we love by faith.

They will also—and this is huge—deny the fact that Jesus is the Son of God (2:22). These are the ones who claim to love the teachings of Jesus, saying that He was a good man, yet they choose to ignore His deity. Jesus said that He and the Father are One, so to deny His identity as the Son of God is to deny God Himself. Father, Son, and Holy Spirit are simply three personalities of one holy God, so you can't have any of these without having them all.

This dark walker will be apathetic to the suffering and needs of others (3:17). God looked on mankind with compassion, seeing our greatest need—a Savior—so He gave us His only begotten Son in order to fill that need (John 3:16). To claim to be a Christian is to also acknowledge that God's Holy Spirit lives in us and works through us.

Therefore, He will point out the needs of others, arranging the times and providing the resources to meet their needs (Ephesians 2:10), and we will cheerfully do this with the same sort of compassion that God has shown us.

Finally (and this is not an exhaustive list), he is lacking in love (4:7). Jesus told His followers that they would be identified as such by the way that they loved one another. It's weird what we've done with the word *love*. It can describe our feelings for a favorite food, team, television show, pet, friend, or family member. The Greeks had different words for different types of love, and the one associated with Christian love is called *agape*. Agape is unearned and unconditional, like the love of a parent for a child. This type of love is not merely an emotion, and it's not simply saying, "I love you." Talk is cheap. Agape takes action. God once again sets the example in John 3:16. It states that God's love was displayed in His actions: God loved and God gave.

The book of 1 John was not intended to make us question our salvation. It was written to help us identify and avoid false teachers, but if you see yourself in some of these passages, then it's time to confess (agree with God about the sin you've stepped in), repent (wash your smelly foot), and resume your walk in the light.

Polecat in the Backyard

Rusty got old, or as the Bible puts it, "advanced in years." He had advanced fourteen years to be exact, and although he was fairly healthy, with old age came certain disabilities. He went through a period of obesity, which contributed to some back problems. These were remedied through bedrest and diet. He also lost some of his vertical leap so that he was no longer able to jump onto a couch or chair. We dealt with this by purchasing some little steps, which we parked next to the couch and ottoman. He also turned into something of a curmudgeon. Some days, I can relate to this. There is no known cure.

These challenges were new to me because most of the dogs I had owned as a kid were claimed by Highway 227 before they had the opportunity to experience old age. The saddest and most impactful effect of Rusty's geriatric state was loss of hearing. We first noticed this when loud noises didn't awaken him. Words that had once excited or frightened him (supper, walk, his name) no longer seemed to affect him at all. We discovered that only a high-pitched whistle could turn his head. Eventually, even that failed to get his attention. Our veterinarian checked his ears and concluded that his hearing loss simply stemmed from getting on in years. Hey, it happens. I understand this better every day.

That's why I was surprised one summer night as we all sat quietly watching TV and recovering from the day. Tina was reading, and Rusty was enjoying a pre-bedtime nap (it's a dachshund thing) when, without warning, he leaped to attention. He jumped from the seat to the arm of the chair and assumed a pride rock pose. The fur along his spine bristled. His ears rose from their resting position. A low growl formed in his throat and was followed by a sudden barking frenzy. Tina and I exchanged puzzled looks.

He hears something; it's a miracle! I thought excitedly.

I winced, concerned for his fragile back, as he leaped from the chair to the ottoman, then down to the floor, bypassing his steps. He scurried to the backdoor, where he danced enthusiastically. I jumped up to let him out, but as

I opened the door, I immediately realized that Rusty had, in fact, not miraculously regained his hearing. His state of red alert was actually due to his sense of smell.

The pungent aroma of polecat (skunk for my Yankee readers) invaded our formerly sweet-smelling home. I scanned the backyard for any sign of a striped, stinky marauder. Seeing nothing within the fence, I decided to indulge Rusty and let him bark. Meanwhile, he had assumed a defensive position at the edge of the porch, from which he scolded the would-be invader, making his stand like Gandalf facing the Balrog and declaring, "You SHALL NOT PASS!" Then, satisfied that he had properly defended his kingdom, he came back in proudly strutting like a conquering hero and resumed his spot on the chair beside Tina. In no time, he was back in dreamland.

Taking care of us humans must be exhausting.

"Ugh, shut the door," Tina said. "That's awful!"

"Well, he's deaf as a post, but his nose is as sharp as ever," I observed. "If it smells bad to us, can you imagine how offensive it must smell to him?"

The rest of the evening passed peacefully, and I didn't give the incident much more thought until the next morning when I was in the shower—I do my best thinking there. I chuckled, recalling how bravely Rusty had charged into the night. I began to reflect on how he had been offended by the odor before Tina and I were even aware of it. Scientists and veterinarians tell us that a dog's nose is thousands of times more sensitive than our own. Any hunter can confirm this fact, and they train their dogs to sniff out quail or other game. Without the dog to guide him, he can't find the birds. The best he could hope for is to stumble onto a covey, but when that happens, he is usually unprepared to aim and fire on them.

As I stood there with the water running over me, I began to see what God wanted to show me through this incident. The polecat smell represents our sin. Many preachers today avoid the subject of sin, preferring to give flowery discourses on love or encouragement. While these topics certainly have a place in biblical education, the subject of sin must not be neglected. Scripture is full of colorful descriptions of how God views our sins, using terms like *detestable*, *abomination*, or *depraved*. Ever since the fall of mankind in the garden of Eden, sin has separated us from Him. The problem is so serious that restoration of our perfect relationship to God required the atoning sacrifice of His Son on the cross.

Sadly, we become numb to the sin surrounding us the same way that we become nose-blind to a foul odor to which we're frequently exposed. Somewhere along the way, we transition from tolerating sin to accepting sin to eventually embracing sin. Hebrews 13:8 tells us, "Jesus Christ is the same yesterday, and today and forever," so from God's point of view, sin still stinks. He never gets used to it, and as we mature in our faith, adopting His mindset, it should become a stench in our spiritual nostrils as well, whether it's our own sin or the sinful state of the world around us.

Jesus prayed for us on the night before His crucifixion because He knew that we would have to live within a world that is infected with sin (John 17:15). He foresaw the balancing act that we would endure, namely living within it without becoming infected by it and without also becoming nose-blind to it, as is too often the case.

That's not to say that we have become completely oblivious to the sin of the world, but we often have to have it hit us in the face before we are offended by it, just as Tina and I had to have the door opened before being offended by the polecat stench. We see the ways that sin ruins lives, and we are saddened by its consequences, especially when those consequences affect those whom we love. We see it whenever we turn on the news or scroll through our social media. We are made aware of it through conversations with friends and coworkers, and it encompasses everything from terrorism to lying, from theft to murder. We grieve over things like crime statistics, drug use, disregard for human life, and human trafficking, and we grumble on Sunday mornings within our churches that the world is "going to Hell in a handbasket."

The observation that we should be making is that it's happening on our watch. If we really want to see the world change, then we must introduce the world to the only one who can change it. God has saved us for the purpose of doing good works (Ephesians 2:10). These works will include benevolence, encouragement, and prayer, but our works must not stop there. We are commanded to share the gospel message (Matthew 28:19; 1 Peter 3:15), and a basic part of that message is that we're all sinners in need of a savior (Romans 3:23). If we never preach against sin, or worse, accept sin into our own lifestyles, we fail in our mission of making disciples and strain our own fellowship with God.

This leads to the subject of another type of sin called *omission*. James 4:17 describes omission plainly: "So whoever knows the right thing to do and fails to do it, for him it is sin."

That's right, sin is not only the "thou shalt nots." Just as important are the "thou shalts." All believers will experience promptings from God to take action in some way. Many of these prompts will come from scripture, while others may come from the sudden awareness of a need. When this happens, we have a choice: either obey or rebel. Our peace with God and our spiritual growth (although not our salvation) depend on which we choose.

I know this not only because I've read it in scripture. I've also experienced it personally. Several months after I was saved, God spoke to me through the book of Ezekiel. We were vacationing in Pigeon Forge, and I woke up before anyone else in the hotel room. As an immature Christian, I had neglected to pack a Bible, so I read from the Gideon copy I found in the nightstand drawer. Have you ever studied the book of Ezekiel? He witnessed some weird, freaky visions—real *X-Files* stuff. There were strange creatures with multiple wings, faces, and wheels! Then God gave him a job to do, sending him to preach a message of repentance. I marveled at what I had read, and I prayed, praising God for what He had shown me.

"That's so cool!" I said. *Lord, I wish that you would speak to me in some unmistakable way and give me a job to do just as you did for him.* People often say to be careful of what you pray for, but in hindsight, I'm glad that I wasn't careful. God had a blessing in store for me.

When we returned home that evening, I attended a Vacation Bible School planning meeting at church. I figured I'd volunteer to park cars or serve Kool-Aid to the kids.

"I'll do whatever needs doing," I said.

"Great," replied our pastor, Mel Johnson. "We need a teacher."

I was dumbfounded for a few seconds, amazed at how God had chosen to answer my morning prayer. I also knew I was faced with a choice of whether to accept or refuse God's call. I was a little hesitant. After all, I had never taught anyone how to do anything, but to refuse would have been a sin of omission. All the way home, I laughed like a lunatic while praying, not for an ability to teach but for God to actually teach through me. That VBS week gave me the opportunity to get to know my church family in a way that only comes from shared work. I felt a sudden need to study and pray more than ever before. God interrupted my sleep with lesson ideas, and I got to witness seventeen kids being saved that week.

You'd think that someone who had experienced such a blessing would have always continued to obey perfectly when God prompted him to do good works. Sadly, such is not the case. Many times, I have allowed recreation, work, family, or just plain laziness to come before my own obedience. In committing the sin of omission, I disappointed God and cheated myself out of a supernatural experience. Thank God for grace, mercy, and second chances.

God also used Rusty to teach me about so-called secret sin.

When we moved to our house in Crossville, we decided that the carpet had to go. It was a nasty combination of black Berber and golden retriever fur, and while we would have preferred hardwood flooring, monetary limitations only allowed for more carpeting. Our choice was a light-brown medium shag, which served its purpose for many years.

Then along came Rusty. He wasn't terribly difficult to house-train. At first, we would simply take him out to the backyard and wait patiently for the magic to happen. When it finally came to pass (pun intended), he was rewarded with praise and a treat. When he got older, we put a harness on him and walked him around the subdivision where we lived. For some reason, he hated this, but it still produced the desired effect. Of course, there were occasional accidents, but as a general rule, our carpets remained unstained. However, this arrangement would not last into his old age.

Still, he did pretty well for an elderly dog—or so we thought.

The carpet began to show signs of wear and tear, and we had discovered a new type of floor covering called vinyl plank. It resembled hardwood but cost significantly less. There was another advantage: I could do much of the installation myself with the aid of my carpenter brothers. Although my skills in such endeavors are somewhat lacking, I could accomplish most of the prep work before they showed up, thus giving us a head start. This included moving out the furniture, ripping up the old carpet and tack strips, then pulling out or grinding down any remaining nails. As I began pulling up the carpet, I soon realized something I had suspected all along: Rusty was not as house-trained as we had hoped. I discovered a wet, stained spot directly behind my chair in an inconspicuous place where nobody usually walked. It was disturbing to realize that we had been living with this disgusting filth right under our feet.

I know that it seems weird, but God used this event to illustrate to me the dangers of so-called secret sin. Rusty had known that he was not supposed to do a certain thing (pee in the house), but he had found a way to hide his misdeed. It seemed to be a pretty good plan until he was discovered.

The same sort of thing happened to King David in 2 Samuel, chapters 11 and 12. He abused his God-given position of power to take another man's wife for himself. The affair resulted in pregnancy. Then he sent her husband to the front lines of battle, where he was certain to be killed. This enabled him to take her as his own wife—problem solved.

However, there was a flaw in his plan.

According to the ending of chapter 11, his adultery, murder, and cover-up "displeased the Lord." By this time, David was so far out of fellowship with God that He had to communicate His displeasure by means of a prophet named Nathan. Nathan told David a story about a rich man with many sheep who took the only sheep of his neighbor, a poor man. King David was enraged at the injustice, declaring that the rich man was not fit to live. Then Nathan hit him with the word from God: "You are the man." David recognized his sin and prayed for forgiveness, which God graciously granted, but tragically, the child produced by the affair died. This is a sobering lesson. If a good man like David, someone God called "a man after his own heart" (1 Samuel 13:14), can fall into the trap of secret sin, then we are also susceptible.

Jesus noted the same type of sin in the lives of the Pharisees of that time. These were supposed to be men of God, holy in conduct, and experts in the law of Moses. People respected them and sought to imitate their behavior, but Jesus saw right through their facade. He publicly revealed their secret sins in Matthew chapter 23, and in verse 25, he said that they washed only the outside of a cup while leaving the inside dirty.

Fast forward to today, and we can see this same hypocrisy is alive and well in the lives of many churchgoers. They sit dutifully in the pews on Sunday morning, yet they don't actually worship. For them, church is a place to make business contacts or simply a place to go because it is socially expected of them. During the rest of the week, they never worship alone or read from a Bible. They never seek God's direction for their lives, trusting instead on their own wits. They present a good front (the outside of the cup), but when they are out of the public eye, they indulge in their own secret sins (the inside of the cup). These sins may include lust, hatred, envy, malice, or any other sin that originates in the heart. It may even involve pornography, adultery, theft, or fraud.

It all raises the question of why anyone would choose to say one thing while actually living and believing another. It can only stem from a lack of faith coupled with a lack of reverential fear of God. Hebrews 11:6 explains this point: "And without faith it is impossible to please him, for whoever would draw near to God must believe that he exists and that he rewards those who seek him."

I don't fear a monster under my bed because I don't really believe that one exists. However, I am concerned about terrorist sleeper cells in this country because I do believe that they exist. See the difference? The way that I think, speak, and act is evidence of either my belief or my unbelief in these matters. People don't always live out the ideals that they espouse, but they will live out what they actually believe, which brings us back to the subject of secret sin.

In Psalm 139, David writes that there is nowhere that we can go where God is not present, nor is there anything that we can say or think that God doesn't know. Jesus mirrored this statement of fact at the end of the book of Matthew when He promised to always be with His disciples. If I don't believe these biblical truths, then I will follow my sinful impulses as long as no one is around to see me, but if I really do believe God's word, then I must live, think, and speak with an awareness of His presence.

In practical terms, this means Jesus sits on the couch beside me as I pick up the remote control. When I turn on my computer, He looks over my shoulder at the screen. He goes to work with me and watches as I either work diligently or slack off. He hears my conversations with my friends or coworkers, and He listens as I either backstab or encourage; gossip or pray; lie or speak truthfully. He observes my obedience or my rebellion as I either follow His leadership or fail to follow Him in the way that I should testify, pray, or exhort others. He goes to church with me, and there He examines my heart. Am I really worshiping, or am I just going through the motions while pondering lunch? Is my service motivated by love for God, or am I looking for applause?

In 1 Samuel 16:7, we learn that while man looks at the outward appearance, God sees the heart. This attribute of God should serve as both a comfort and a warning. He loves us and knows our motives. He understands what makes us tick in a way that no human friend, brother, or spouse ever could. This is explained in John 2:25: "Jesus needed no one to bear witness about man, for he himself knew what was in man."

He also explained to His disciples in Matthew 10:26 that there is nothing "covered that will not be revealed." Rusty's pee-stained carpet reveals this fact. There really is no such thing as a secret sin.

So who's to blame for the things that we do, don't do, or that we think are hidden? Once again, Rusty taught me something about the nature of God.

We left the house in a hurry one morning and had neglected to put out a puppy pad. We returned home that afternoon to a mess, but we couldn't really blame Rusty too much. After all, we had set him up to fail.

Many people attempt to blame God for the sins they commit, claiming that they were created with certain weaknesses therefore, like Rusty, were predestined to fail. This mindset shifts blame and eliminates personal responsibility. It's a cop-out, and James refutes it in chapter 1 of his letter to the churches, wherein he tells us that God is not tempted to sin, nor does He tempt anyone. Our temptations arise from our evil desires. That's why Jesus said in Luke 11:4 that we should pray not to be led into temptation and to be delivered from the evil one. Furthermore, in 1 Corinthians 10:13, we are promised that God will always provide us an escape from temptation, so when a Christian sins, it is a deliberate choice. We can't sincerely pray for God not to lead us into temptation when we go looking for it on our own. Just as Rusty couldn't blame anyone else for his carpet stain, neither can we blame anyone else for our sin. We must allow God to pull back the carpet to expose it to our own conscience, thus allowing Him to replace it with something new and much better. He loved us enough to die on the cross as an atonement for our smelly sin, omission sin, hypocrisy sin, and hidden sin. We can stray far from God through these sins, but all that's required to return is a single step of repentance. He's waiting.

GOD'S WISDOM VS MAN'S AND MAN'S WISDOM VS DOG'S

When Rusty was just a pup, we took him with us to visit my sister Carol, who had a little dog of her own. Jack was a small Jack Russell terrier (yes, I, too, thought the name lacked imagination), whom they had owned for several years. I was curious as to how the dogs would interact, as the only other dogs Rusty had known were his littermates.

We piled out of the van and found Carol relaxing on her screened-in back porch with a paperback novel. Jack was content to lie at her feet.

"You brought the rusty puppy," she exclaimed excitedly. Jack looked on, curious but not hostile. Rusty was wide-eyed and interested, his tail wagging as she took him onto her lap. Upon seeing this, Jack jumped into the chair and took a long inhalation in the direction of Rusty's posterior.

"Jack," she chided, "don't be an ol' butt sniffer."

Have you ever wondered why an animal with such a keen sense of smell would choose to sniff another dog's rear end? A quick Google search tells us that they are gathering information about the other dog. A sniff can inform them of the other dog's gender, diet, and even their state of mind. The more that they know about their newly-met canine brother, the better they are equipped to know how to behave around him. Does he want to play? Will he lead to good food? Is he aggressive? Is he sick? Information leads to knowledge, and knowledge leads to wisdom, ideally. People follow the same pattern of information gathering. Thankfully, we do it without the butt-sniffing, although that might be more accurate than the goofy questions we ask one another.

"What do you do for a living?" Have you ever wondered why it's one of the first questions we ask when we meet someone? It's a time-tested icebreaker, small talk, but that's not the only reason we ask it. We have a need to assess the other person and find out what makes them who they are and what makes them tick. We might follow up with questions about his hometown, family, or even (War Eagle) his favorite team. Amassing information this way arms us with the knowledge of how to interact with this person.

Unfortunately, we also use this information to make judgments, and we might even form opinions about his worth. For instance, if his answer is neurosurgeon, we instantly conjure mental images of his daily work. We imagine the labor and commitment it must have taken to earn his degree and position. We assume that this person is hardworking, dedicated, intelligent, and compassionate. Surely, he is wealthy. He must have a beautiful home and drive a new car. His wife and family probably resemble a postcard. He is happy and fulfilled, isn't he? In fact, we really have no clue about this man. Instead of being happy, he may be facing a messed-up life filled with regret. He may have issues like depression, loneliness, or addiction. He may be in the middle of a divorce. Maybe someone he loves has just died. He could be up to his eyeballs in debt.

On the other hand, suppose his answer is sanitation worker. We will probably make many different assumptions about this person. We might see him as an underachiever. Did he even finish high school? Is he literate? Surely, he's not very bright. Is he married, and can he afford to raise children? Poor soul, he must be miserable, right? Again, we don't really know the answer to that question. Perhaps his idea of wealth is not based on money. His job may allow him time off to enjoy hobbies and family time that other careers would, by their demanding nature, prohibit. He could even be one of those secret millionaires about whom we read in the tabloids!

The fact is that we simply don't have all the information needed to make any sort of judgment on the work ethics, upbringing, lifestyle, or state of mind of these people. We have seen one aspect of their lives, and in our arrogance, we have considered ourselves capable of drawing conclusions about them. We make the same sort of assessments based on appearance and possessions, and we declare this person to be either a success or failure. It's not unlike seeing one side of a Rubik's cube solved and assuming that the rest of the cube is complete as well. All the while, we deem ourselves wise enough to judge this person when we have actually proven ourselves to be foolish.

God's ideas about wisdom, foolishness, success, and failure are far different from ours, and one reason for this is that He sees the whole picture. His knowledge and vision are without limitation, while ours are constrained by our humanity. We are pitiful by comparison. In his first letter to the church at Corinth, Paul described the contrast: "Where is the one who is wise? Where is the scribe? Where is the debater of this age? Has not God made foolish the wisdom of the world?" (1 Corinthians 1:20).

Once again, God used Rusty to help me understand this basic truth.

Rusty's typical day begins with waking me early—usually around four o'clock—so that he can go outside to answer nature's call. (Sometimes he doesn't need to go out. He just gets lonely and wants someone to keep him company.) After he watches me stumble out of bed, he sits and observes me attentively as I cook my breakfast, hoping to get a bite. (Of course, he will.) After this, he usually retires back to sleep on the couch until it's time for his own breakfast, which, of course, makes another backyard trip necessary. He sleeps most of the day while we're at work until his internal clock tells him it's time for our return. When he sees our cars pull into the driveway, he begins to whine and dance excitedly, and he runs to the door to greet us. This usually earns him a pat on the head and some sort of baby-voiced greeting.

Sometimes we play. He likes to fetch a ball or play tug-of-war with a rope. Jada taught him a few tricks when he was just a pup, and he still remembers them. On command, he sits, rolls over, jumps, lies down, and speaks. The successful performance of these tasks earns him a treat to tide him over until suppertime. He gobbles this up as though he will never eat again, and soon afterward, he requires another trip outside. During the summer months, he usually stays out while we attend to various yard work. The end of the day means relaxing beside Tina in an oversized chair, where he waits for her to get a snack. She allows him to lick the residual yogurt from the cup when she's finished. Soon, it's bedtime, and the cycle repeats.

It sounds pretty boring, right? Yet this is his life. He lives in a very limited world compared to that of his masters. He is totally ignorant of where we go or what we do when we leave every day. He knows nothing about politics (lucky dog), the economy, news, sports, or anything else that happens outside his house or backyard. (This is not withstanding occasional walks or trips to the vet or groomer, all of which he hates.) His life revolves around his basic needs, yet if he possessed any self-awareness, he would probably consider himself to be successful and wise.

All of his accomplishments actually amount to very little in the grand scheme of things. They're not unlike the "stupid pet tricks" one can watch online. Oh, we're mildly entertained for a few minutes, and he does manage to earn a treat or two. He understands how to avoid scolding by not getting into the trash or not relieving himself indoors. Still, we can see that his efforts don't really make a difference in the world. From our point of view, all his endeavors are not wise. In fact, they are truly quite pointless. I guess we must have wanted him that way, or we would have trained him to do other things. As he is, he is quite ineffective (this book notwithstanding).

He didn't have to turn out this way. Many dogs throughout history have done very important, sometimes heroic, work. They serve as guides for the blind. They can predict seizures in people who suffer from epilepsy. They sniff out drugs or explosives in airports or for the police. They can find earthquake victims buried in rubble, track criminals on the run, locate cadavers, tree raccoons, fetch downed quail, or guard property. Just as Rusty is unaware of his ineffectiveness, these dogs don't realize that they are making the world a better place. They do these things in obedience to commands. Their only real wisdom comes in the form of faith in their masters, who understand the importance of the work that they have assigned and have only their best interests in mind. Their faith in their masters is evident in their obedience.

God's word teaches us the same truth about genuine wisdom and success. Psalm 111:10 tells us that real wisdom begins with a healthy fear (respect, reverence, and awe that inspires obedience) of God, and Psalm 14:1 tells us that the one who denies the existence of God is a fool. We understand that our behaviors are reflections of our beliefs, so if we really believe that God exists and earnestly rewards those who seek Him (Hebrews 11:6), then we will strive to live in obedience to His commands. As a wise philosopher once said, "Stupid is as stupid does" (*Forrest Gump*). The same holds true for wisdom.

Therefore, a question looms before me. Am I wise, or am I foolish? I'm incapable of realistically making this judgment on my own, as I am hardly unbiased. Instead, I must submit to God's assessment of my wisdom or foolishness, my success or failure. Of course, Jesus explained this best in Matthew 7:24–27:

> Everyone then who hears these words of mine and does them will be like a wise man who built his house on the rock. And the rain fell, and the floods came, and the winds blew and beat on that house, but it did not fall, because it had been founded on the rock. And everyone who hears these words of mine and does not do them will be like a foolish man who built his house on the sand. And the rain fell, and the floods came, and the winds blew and beat against that house, and it fell, and great was the fall of it.

From this passage, we can determine that the wise man is the one who builds his life on his relationship with God rather than trusting in his own wisdom. He also trusts God to know what is truly good or evil, forsaking his own opinions about such matters. As a result, his good works are truly good. He is successful, and he is wise.

In contrast, the foolish man will continue to judge his own self-worth. He will forsake the actual God and become a deity to himself, determining his own ideas of right and wrong, wealth and poverty, success and failure. The foolish man will not live by faith. Instead, he will attempt to possess all that this world has to offer because he believes that this world is all that exists. Jesus warned us about this mindset in Matthew 6:19–20: "Do not lay up for yourselves treasures on earth, where moth and rust destroy and where thieves break in and steal, but lay up for yourselves treasures in heaven, where neither moth nor rust destroys and where thieves do not break in and steal."

From this passage, as well as from the preceding and following scripture, we learn that man's idea of wisdom (accumulation of money and possessions) is what is seen and approved by himself and his peers, whereas God's idea of wisdom (faith and obedience) is known only to God. Additional support for this doctrine can be found in the parable of a foolish rich man in Luke 12:18–21. Therein is described a foolish man who accumulated worldly wealth while ignoring the condition of his own soul.

The Apostle Paul repeated this doctrine to the church at Corinth in 1 Corinthians 2:6–7. At that time, there were great debates about wisdom. The Epicureans argued with the Stoics. The Pharisees argued with the Sadducees. Similarly, we see debates rage in our present day among different sects of religion, and there is no lack of hostility between political parties. In fact, anyone looking for a fight has only to offer a point of view about almost any topic ranging from sports, fashion, economics, or entertainment. Their social media posts almost instantly "blow up" with opposing viewpoints and opinions.

Each of these influencers considers himself wise. Meanwhile, God looks at all this from an omniscient, sovereign, and timeless viewpoint. He sees our opinions for the foolishness that they really are. He watches as we plan and scheme different ways to improve our world and solve all the problems of mankind. He must surely shake His head as He hears us discuss just the right government leader, just the right social program, or just the right personal path to fulfillment when He has already identified mankind's biggest problem: sin. He has also already given us the only real solution for that problem: His Son.

Stop and think about God's wisdom for a moment. In His wisdom, He created a perfect, sinless universe and declared it "good." There was no strife, crime, poverty, or injustice. The fantasy of utopia was a reality. Best of all, man and God existed in perfect fellowship, unhampered by sin. You know the rest of the story. The serpent tempted Eve. She and Adam ate the fruit that God had forbidden, and mankind began to develop their own ideas of morality, wisdom, and purpose. The serpent had told Eve that she would become "like God, knowing right from wrong," but he failed to mention that her viewpoints would be limited and therefore flawed. (He also failed to mention the consequences of sin and God's judgment.)

It's easy to be a Monday-morning quarterback, but I know myself well enough to know that I would have made the same mistake as Eve. Sometimes, my decisions reflect a deep-seated belief that I know better than God what's best for me. It's also preached in the secular world, which tells each of us to live our own truth. What's right for one is wrong for another. You do you. Throughout history, this foolishness has resulted in countless conflicts among nations, within churches, in families, and even inside our own minds. It's comparable to the mess that would result from a crew of carpenters who each had their own viewpoint on the length of an inch. Nobody in his right mind would want to live in the house (or world) built by such a group.

We can't, however, make the mistake of thinking that all our problems as a society can be solved with like-minded thinking. We can all be headed in the same direction and still be going the wrong way. Many dictators throughout history have proven this point. If we are to live both as united and wise, then our leader must be perfect, righteous, and just, but this presents us with another problem: we are flawed people who are incapable of following perfectly. Thus, the leader must also be compassionate and able to forgive us when we fail. This conundrum of a perfect, wise God who wants to have a relationship with a flawed, foolish human race could only be solved by God Himself. His Son bridged the gap between the two, enabling us to become people who follow Him. We follow by faith, and our work proves to be wise, even if the world sees it as foolish. This faith requires us to trust in God just as a good dog trusts his master.

And aren't we better off living by faith rather than by sight? After all, my sight is quite limited. I see only a small slice of time and space in the same way that Rusty sees only as far as his backyard. What God sees is without the limits imposed by an eighty-year lifespan and a nine-to-five job. What He thinks and how He weaves together our destinies is beyond my comprehension. No life coach for me, thanks. I have the only one I'll ever need.

Epilogue

I've struggled to write an ending for this book. Books about dogs traditionally end sadly, as in the cases of *Old Yeller* or *Where the Red Fern Grows*, but as I write this epilogue, Rusty is still with us, snoozing contentedly under his blanket on the couch, *his couch.* He claimed this spot as a pup and has never relinquished it.

I recently attempted to sleep there when the little monster awakened me at 3:00 a.m. He was well aware that it was too early for breakfast. I suppose he just got lonely. I, on the other hand, was irritated and groggy. I needed more sleep, so I set the alarm on my phone, searched YouTube for rain noises, and laid down on the couch with Rusty. Two hours later, I awoke somewhat refreshed but also slightly disgusted as I realized that I was covered in dog hair. I lay there thinking about this nasty circumstance and wondering how such a small dog could produce so much hair. How was it possible that he wasn't bald? My poor couch—it would never come clean. This shed dog hair would outlive Rusty (and probably us as well).

It was at this moment that God spoke to me, and I realized that we all "shed" something in this life, leaving parts of ourselves for others to find after we are gone. We shed words, actions, and attitudes. All of these can either be beneficial or hurtful. They "cover" our families, friends, and coworkers as memories in much the same way that Rusty's shed hair covered me. We affect the world that we leave behind, just as Rusty has forever affected my couch.

This begs the question: What am I shedding? Money is eventually spent. Possessions usually end up in a donation bin. Even memories and funny stories are eventually forgotten. Instead of focusing on worldly things, I should instead strive to leave a legacy of faith because acts of faith have far-reaching effects on the world. The Bible tells us that the faith of Abel—one of Adam and Eve's sons—still speaks (Hebrews 11). The Apostle Paul also left this type of legacy, and he described it to his protege Timothy in 2 Timothy 4:6–7. Bear in mind that these are the words of a man writing from a Roman prison and facing his impending execution.

> For I am already being poured out like a drink offering, and the time of my departure has come. I have fought the good fight, I have finished the race, I have kept the faith.

Isn't that all that really matters?

ABOUT THE AUTHOR

Chuck Hester is a letter carrier for the United States Postal Service. He lives in Crossville, Alabama, and attends First Baptist Church of Geraldine. In addition to teaching Sunday school, he enjoys singing in the church choir as well as participating in a community choir called the Mountain Valley Singers. A free afternoon will find him riding his bicycle, working out at the gym, or simply relaxing in his back porch hammock in the good company of Rusty, the wiener dog. Chuck and his wife, Tina, visit their children, Zach and Jada, whenever the opportunity arises.